# Indonesia's
# SIX YEARS
## of Living Dangerously
### From Habibie Through Gus Dur To Megawati

## *Will Yudhoyono Succeed?*

### J.F.Conceicao

Horizon Books
Singapore • Kuala Lumpur
www.horizonbooks.com.sg

First published in 2005 by


HORIZON BOOKS PTE LTD
Block 5 Ang Mo Kio Industrial Park 2A
#05-12/14 AMK Tech II
Singapore 567760
E-mail: horizon@horizonbooks.com.sg


HORIZON BOOKS SDN BHD
Wisma Yeoh Tiong Tee
72C Jalan Sungai Besi
57100 Kuala Lumpur
Malaysia
E-mail: horizon@wismaytt.com

Cover design: Cheryl Marie Song

ISBN 981-05-2307-6

# CONTENTS

# PREFACE

This composition on Indonesia's difficult, even tumultuous half-a-dozen years, between the fall of Suharto and the exit of Megawati, comes not from any expert pen or that of scholarship. Having been posted to Jakarta as Singapore's ambassador, I was simply interested, as one who discovered affection for Indonesia, in the post-Suharto events that attended the swift rise and demise of the country's trial leaders.

This work has therefore been a very lay effort. I got the term "years of living dangerously", as others did from charismatic Sukarno's magnetic self-proclamation on Indonesia's national day in 1964, that *that* was Indonesia's year of "*vivere periculoso*" – rather perilous Italian for – "living dangerously".

1964 was the year when Sukarno threatened to *ganyang* Malaysia, that is to chew and spit it out, when he mounted Confrontation against his country's neighbour. It was also the end of 1964 when Sukarno took Indonesia out of the UN. He wanted to form a conference of newly emerging forces which Indonesia and other countries of like mettle could join. The year 1964 was also the year preceding the sad and infamous Gestapu, the *Gerakan September Tiga Puloh*, the September 30 Movement of 1965. The fantastic blood-bath which resulted from Gestapu triggered the fall of Sukarno.

Suharto took over and rode the consequences which Sukarno had unwittingly unleashed. He was lucky in the succession and changeover of generals and economic czar-counsellors who stood by his side over the next thirty or so years. The saga of Sofyan Wanandi was symbolic and symptomatic of such transformation. He was, with his brother Yusuf, an important leader in the Centre for Strategic and International Studies (CSIS), which helped Suharto with intelligence, in the fight against communism. The CSIS was also, throughout almost two-thirds of Suharto's regime, highly favoured by Murtopo, Benny Murdani and Humardani, all generals close to Suharto.

This period was coincidental with Indonesia's rising prosperity, in which Chinese Indonesians played a high-profile role. The high price of oil and inordinately high interest rates were features that encouraged a large inflow of capital. But the balance of influence tilted towards resentful Muslim leaders who complained against what they saw as excesses of the privileged classes. New generals and new advisers came to the fore. Sofyan Wanandi came under scrutiny for alleged involvement in a bomb plot. History was turning a full circle.

Suharto's innings drew swifly to a close. The economic crisis of 1997, already preceded by sporadic violence against Christians and Chinese, triggered uncontrollable rioting, in which students joined in. With Indonesia and the world appalled by plunder and rape against the Chinese and the shooting of students, Suharto stepped down in 1998.

# WHO'S WHO IN INDONESIA

Indonesian politics involves a pantheon of players, political parties and institutions. The following list, by no means comprehensive, gives thumbnail sketches of important figures and groups mentioned in the book.

**Hari Sabarno.** Appointed by Megawati, in March 2004, to be Coordinating Minister for Social and Political Affairs, *ad interim*, taking Susilo Bambang Yudhoyono's place when the latter stepped down to contest the 2004 presidential elections. Sabarno had previously been Home Affairs minister.

**Agus Widjoyo,** Lieutenant-General: At one time head of the military representation in the Indonesian parliament, until the military withdrew such representation. Widjoyo had also held the post of head of the military's territorial bureau.

**Henry Dunant Centre:** Humanitarian centre, involved in trying to bring about peace between the Indonesian government and the Free Aceh Movement (GAM). Its efforts were unsuccessful.

**Agus Wirahadikusuma,** Lieutenant-General: Such an enthusiastic reformer in the military, that he caused anxiety among many senior generals, because they thought he was proceeding too hastily. His death came prematurely. Outspoken, he once accused radical elements of the military of involvement in the creation of Laskar Jihad (Forces for Holy War) to de-stabilise the government (during Abdurrahman Wahid's term).

**Prabowo Subianto.** A retired lieutenant-general and former Special Forces (Kopassus) chief, he was accused of fomenting the 1998 riots which led to Suharto's downfall – although he vigorously denied this. Former military chief, General Wiranto, brought honour-court investigations against him for misinterpreting orders, and discharged him from the military. Prabowo was married to Titiek, second daughter of Suharto. But the fallen First Family apparently disowned him.

**Association of Muslim Intellectuals (ICMI):** At first, Suharto discouraged Islam's politicisation. In the early days he depended on a group of Indonesian activists, mostly Chinese Christian, whose Centre for Security and International Studies was also encouraged by Suharto generals, Murtopo and Benny Murdani. The influence of such a group faded with the passage of years. Suharto decided to pay attention to offended Muslim feeling. He encouraged his protègè Habibie to form the ICMI. But the ICMI was only one way of expanding Muslim interests, which also included the fostering of the Haj pilgrimage, building of mosques, even the setting up of banks. The ICMI was also one of Suharto's means of curbing his red (nationalist) against his green (Islam-favouring) generals.

**Murtopo, General:** Suharto's most trusted intelligence chief and political adviser, right up until Murtopo's death. Murtopo encouraged activists from the Centre for Strategic and International Studies in their support for Suharto, after the attempted communist coup in 1965. Such activists provided intelligence gathered from Christian locations all over Indonesia, and also took part in agitation and demonstrations against communism. Murtopo was also well-known for his successful "coup" against General Sumitro who had been a frequent critic of Suharto. Murtopo succeeded in putting the blame for the 1974 so-called *malari* anti-Japanese riots squarely on Sumitro.

**Pemuda Pancasila:** A youth organisation, allegedly set up to provide education and training for unemployed youths. But PP was also known to have produced "heavies" to assist the government side in election activities.

**ABRI:** Initials for *Angkatan Bersenjata Republik Indonesia* or the Armed Forces of the Republic of Indonesia.

*ABRI masok desa*: ABRI enters the village. Colloquial way of expressing ABRI's *dwi-fungsi* (dual function) or additional political role. This described the territorial activities of the armed forces, which positioned selected officers in parallel positions to officials of the civilian government. The rank of the military representatives would be graduated according to the ranking level of the civilian match. Democratic agitation against such military intervention in the civilian administration resulted in a withdrawal of such a system, particularly after ABRI's designation was changed to TNI. But custom being rooted, remnants of the territorial system still remained.

**TNI: Tentara Nasional Indonesia** or the Indonesian National Army. This was to differentiate the army from the police force, which had previously been part of ABRI.

**Adi Sasono:** Habibie's Cooperatives Minister. Was also a participant of the ICMI which Habibie had initiated. Sasono formed an organisation called the People's Centre for the Economy (*Pusat Ekonomi Rakyat*). He was strenuously against Chinese control of (portions of) Indonesia's economy, and fulminated on this theme, although he denied he was anti-Chinese *per se*. On the positive side he was known to have encouraged the development of indigenous small-scale entrepreneurs.

**Wiranto, General.** Commander-in-chief of the armed forces, he had been close to Suharto as Adjutant. He was ambitious to take over after Suharto's fall. Allegedly, he hoped to be vice-president to Megawati, so he could be the power behind her. But with Gus Dur's ascension, he consented to the cabinet post of Coordinating Minister for Defence and Security. He was later accused of involvement in the violence that occurred after Timor's bid for independence – an allegation he denied. His story is about how he fell from power, and rose to be a candidate in a presidential election.

*Poros tengah:* A central axis ( loose grouping) of Islamic forces was gathered, and gathered influence, before the election of Abdurrahman Wahid to the presidency. It also included the United Development Party (PPP), the National Mandate Party (PAN), and the Crescent Star Party (PBB). One purpose of this coalition was to express a certain Islamic preference, against the secular and female candidature of Megawati, and for Wahid as the more likeable Muslim candidate. One of the main organisers was Amien Rais of PAN.

*Pancasila:* National philosophy first espoused by Sukarno, consisting of five principles – humanism, nationalism, consultative government by the people, national unity and monotheism or belief in one God.

**Rudini:** Retired general and former Home Affairs Minister under Suharto. Board member of ICMI. Quiet personality, noted for temperate outlook.

**Hartono:** Former Army chief, Suharto loyalist and close friend of the Suharto family, particularly of Tutut, Suharto's eldest daughter. Was said to have sought the ageing Suharto's permission to take over the running of Golkar, but this was disapproved. Formed a political party (Concern for the Nation Party) to support Tutut as a candidate in the 2004 presidential elections. This also came to naught.

**Sumargono, Ahmad:** Interesting character, about whom contradictory rumours were rife. One was that he was involved in the arrest of Abu Bakar Bashir who was accused of links with the Jemaah Islamiyah, an Islamic terrorist group. This was contradictory to Sumargono's stated position of support for Bashir.

Sumargono was leader of the Indonesian Committee for World Islamic Solidarity (KISDI). He expressed his belief that the Bali bombing was a Western plot to apply pressure on Indonesia to be more pro-West. He supported the enforcement of Islamic law in Indonesia, and loved his role as a radical Islamic hero.

Tutut: Siti Hardiyanti Rukmana, Suharto's eldest daughter, most engaged of her family in the political life of the country. Was for a brief while a minister in her father's last cabinet. Put herself forward as a presidential candidate in the 2004 elections. Well known for interest in charitable work.

Nadlatul Ulama: Largest Muslim organisation in Indonesia, with about 40 million members. Its adherents consisted of a rural membership of those educated and being educated in *pesantrens*, or Islamic boarding institutions. Gus Dur's party, the National Awakening Party (PKB), was based on the Nadlatul Ulama.

Golkar: An abbreviation for *golongan karya*, meaning functional groups. It represented ABRI's efforts to bring together all sorts of adherents – trade unionists, civil servants, and those working in the private sector, under one political umbrella. Golkar was a slip-over from Suharto times, and hence, faced many enemies who wanted to see it dissolved. Internally too, many deserted the rift-torn party. Golkar was alleged to have benefited from the disbursement of Bulog funds. The case was brought to court, but evidence was insufficient to find the party guilty. In the 1999 parliament, Golkar had the highest number of members, of all parties, in the House of Representatives (DPR).

Akbar Tandjung: Golkar chairman and Speaker in Parliament's House of Representatives. He is a controversial figure, having been accused of corruption, sentenced and then successfully appealing against his conviction. Tried to run for president, but his party, Golkar, chose Wiranto instead as their candidate, who' – in any case – did not attain success.

Muhammadiyah: The next largest Muslim organisation, after Nadlatul Ulama, with an estimated membership of 30 million, consisting mainly of urban small and medium businessmen.

Amien Rais: Leader of the National Mandate Party (PAN), and also Parliamentary Speaker in the People's Assembly. He was educated in the US, besides Indonesia. He once led the Muhammadiyah, the country's second-largest Muslim organisation. He left Muhammadiyah to pursue a nationalist role in politics, especially to win over the middle classes, but was not very his successful. Therefore, PAN became more tilted towards Islam. He threw in support behind Gus Dur. Always activistic in the political arena, he then swiftly moved to support Megawati, when Gus Dur proved disappointing. May have entertained presidential ambitions but this too did not seem to have met with success. Perhaps Amien was over-scholarly.

**Hasan di Tiro:** Also has the title of Teuku (the Achenese equivalent of Tengku). Chief of the Free Aceh Movement (GAM or *Gerakan Aceh Merdeka*), but lives in Sweden. Was said to have an unwritten agreement with his hostcountry, in which he has become a citizen, for its support in his determined struggle to secede Aceh from Indonesia. A peace accord was agreed upon in Geneva, in December 2002, between GAM and the Indonesian government, arranged by the Henry Dunant Centre. A GAM representative, Zaini Abdullah, did the signing. Hasan de Tiro did not turn up.

**Hamza Haz:** Leader of the pro-Islamic United Development Party (PPP), one of three political parties Suharto permitted during his regime, the other two being Golkar and the Democratic Party. He was Megawati's vice-president, but showed a radical support for Islamic figures. For instance, he visited imprisoned Umar Thalib, leader of Laskar Jihad. He was a presidential candidate in the 2004 elections, with retired general Agum Gumelar as his running mate.

**PPP:** Partai Persatuan Pembangunan or United Development Party, a carry-over from Suharto's time. It was used to heeding government requests, but at the same time was strongly influenced by Islamic figures. It tried to enter into agreement with Golkar and PDIP to scotch Yudhoyono's chances at the 2004 presidential election but was not successful.

**Djadja Suparman:** A retired lieutenant-general and,, at one time, Head of Strategic Command, he appeared to be a close friend of Wiranto, because they were together accused of being behind the disturbances in Maluku. The accusation was dropped with an apology. But Strategic Command came under financial scrutiny for its economic manipulation. This became a *cause celebre* after Agus Wirahadikusuma took over from Suparman.

**Fachrul Razi,** Lieutenant-General: Former chief of the general staff of the Indonesian armed forces. Became chairman of Wiranto's presidential election team. Was for a while secretary-general in the Ministry of Defence. During Gus Dur's regime, he stoutly proclaimed that there was no military commander who could be disloyal to the government, when Gus Dur raised such a question.

**Marzuki Darusman:** Indonesia's attorney-general. Spent some time in Europe in his youth, and was described as having had a good upbringing. He was a Golkar MP, and served on the Human Rights Commission. He took up the case against Suharto for corruption, and Wiranto for human rights abuse, and caused Bob Hasan to be imprisoned.

**Yuzril Ihza Mahendra:** Was Indonesia's Minister for Justice and Human Rights. Headed the Crescent Star political party (PBB – Partai Bulan Bintang), which had an orientation towards Islam. Supported the Yudhoyono-Yusuf Kalla team in the 2004 presidential elections. Mahendra as Justice Minister, had authority over immigration issues and imposed immigration restrictions which were reciprocal to conditions which other countries imposed on Indonesia, for example, the necessity for visas.

**Fadli Zon:** Executive director at the Institute for Policy Studies, and seen also as a political analyst. Strongly pro-Islam and anti-Christian. Like Kivlan Zein (see below), he wrote a book assigning blame for the 1998 disturbances to Wiranto. Was a crony of Prabowo Subianto who, despite his exterior politeness, must have resented Wiranto, the man responsible for his retirement.

**Kivlan Zein:** retired major-general, and at one time chief of Kostrad, the army strategic command. A friend of Prabowo Subianto. Wrote about the 1998 conflicts and blamed them on General Wiranto. He had previously carried out Wiranto's instructions to form a civilian guards militia to protect parliament from demonstrating students. Seems to have been adept at such operations.

**Bulog:** *Badan Urusan Logistik*, the national foodstuffs distribution monopoly was a well-known Suharto institution, well-known indeed for how the powerful exploited it rather than how the poor fed on it. Its logistics function included controlling the supply of rice and basic commodities. It was said to have supported privileged private economic interests, for such interests to render a *quid pro quo* to economic entities controlled by, for example, the military or the palace itself.

**Bob Hasan:** An Indonesian-Chinese Muslim, variously described as a "timber baron" or an industrialist with wide interests, including mining as well as timber and its products. He was a close friend of Suharto and his frequent golf buddy. He served Suharto for a short while as Minister for Trade and Industry.

# CHAPTER 1

# HABIBIE THE TECHNOCRAT

THREE successive presidents after Suharto attained their presidencies through default. Suharto, Indonesia's strongman for over three decades, was forced to resign in May 1998 – personally beleaguered and politically defeated. The economy had collapsed, there were serious riots, rape and pillaging had occurred in Jakarta, and social unrest was mounting nationwide. There was a suspicion that elements of the military were responsible for instigating chaos, and the behaviour of Suharto's son-in-law, Prabowo Subianto, had given rise to speculation that he was hoping to ride to power in the midst of pandemonium. If he was, it was a miscalculation. Prabowo was bitterly renounced by his own in-laws.

In such adverse circumstances, German-trained technocrat, and Suharto's vice-president, Dr B J Habibie, was handed the presidency. Habibie was later fond of describing himself as president by accident. But this fortuitous accession was greeted by mixed reactions. Of course, the ICMI (the Association of Muslim Intellectuals) would generally be glad that their founder had become the president. And so would elements of Golkar, Indonesia's dominant political party, and Suharto's principal vehicle of political control. But such closeness to the deposed Suharto did not reflect favourably. Moreover, Habibie (technologically brilliant though he may have been) had little experience of economic management.

At first, ABRI headed by General Wiranto, supported Habibie. ABRI or Angkatan Bersenjata Republic Indonesia was Indonesia's armed forces. This was later changed to TNI (Tentara Nasional Indonesia) but it essentially meant the same thing as ABRI. The armed forces followed a philosophy of parallel control as the civil administration. (Coincidentally, when the term TNI was mooted in 1998, Indonesia's recenlty-elected president Susilo Bambang Yudhoyono was a principal supporter. He became head of territorial forces, which meant he was *au fait* with what went on in the territories over which ABRI exercised parallel administration.)

What else could they do? Wiranto knew of Suharto's final reservations that Habibie would not last long. And this about the very person the former president had brought up!

Born in 1936 in Makassar, the young Habibie found in Suharto a godfather, during the latter's military posting there in the 1950s. Suharto encouraged Habibie in his education, until Habibie continued his educational and professional successes in Germany. He became the technical director of a prominent German industrial concern, the Messerschmitt-Bolkow-Blohm aeronautical company, and worked there for many years before he returned to Indonesia.

After Suharto became president, he brought Habibie out of Germany. Habibie owed much of his political career and success in life to Suharto.

President Suharto had his own reasons for nurturing Habibie. Perhaps he had been dazzled by the sparkle-eyed aircraft engineer's plans to catapult Indonesia into the high-tech era. Suharto had also invited Habibie to sponsor the ICMI to strengthen the president's Islamic image.

Habibie was an ardent admirer of the president, to the point of being sycophantic. But on becoming president himself, Habibie pledged to break up the authoritarian system he had inherited. He initiated freedom of the press and political activity. He swiftly put on the mantle of democracy.

But Habibie was politically naïve. In Indonesia's current circumstances at the time, he wanted the country to make a swift transition to *reformasi*. In Indonesia, to be a rational politician was a contradiction in terms. Habibie needed to understand the powerful feelings of nationalism arising out of Indonesia's history, where such feelings largely possessed the Javanese. He had to understand the rural sentiments that moved much of the population, as well as their characteristic loyalty to their Muslim faith.

He had to understand how traditional rural Islam was linked, for example, with Abdurrahman Wahid, popularly known as Gus Dur, leader of the National Awakening Party (PKB). Wahid also had close links with the Nadlatul Ulama (NU), the largest Muslim grouping in Indonesia, reportedly with 40 million followers. The NU organised and managed *pesantrens* or religious schools principally located in rural areas.

Yet Islam had its urban quality too. Habibie had to perceive how urban Muslims looked to Amien Rais, the general-secretary of the National Mandate Party or PAN, or the Muhammadiyah, which regarded itself as a reform movement. The Muhammadiyah was next in the number of followers after the NU, roughly calculated at about 30 million. Many of its adherents were owners or managers of small and medium enterprises, and hence, largely urban dwellers. It had a strong reputation for attracting scholars and intellectuals.

Then there was Megawati Sukarnoputri, Sukarno's daughter, who led the powerful Sukarnoist Indonesian Democratic Party – Struggle or PDI-P.

Habibie did not care about such distribution of political power. He thought all would depend on his past practical performance, which he judged over-optimistically. Nevertheless, Habibie must be remembered as the president who democratised the Indonesian general elections. In doing this, he also strengthened the political positions of the parties which were in opposition to him.

The Constitution had required Habibie as vice-president to take over from President Suharto, when Suharto became incapacitated. It was not the people who had chosen Habibie, but the Rules of the State that had propped him up. He had no political ground to speak of. Habibie became almost bankrupt of political credentials when General Wiranto refused to run as his vice-president.

Yet he declared that he had captured the aspirations of the people. It was an unconvincing statement. Conventional wisdom suggested that someone from Sulawesi, who had spent an important part of his life in Germany, would not achieve this easily. Or was Habibie simply expressing the triumph of his hopes?

He stressed his commitment to shape a government that was clean, and free from corruption, collusion and nepotism (KKN). But, despite jettisoning obvious Suharto favourites, like Fuad Bawazier (an old crony of Suharto's, who had served him as finance minister) and Bob Hasan (reputedly the closest confidant Suharto ever entertained, and a frequent golf partner) as well as Suharto's daughter Tutut, two-thirds of Habibie's cabinet were previous Suharto office-holders.

It was also said that Habibie had placed his eldest son Akbar in virtual charge of the Nusantara Aircraft Manufacturing Industry (IPTN= Industri Pesawat Terbang Nusantara) while the Batam Development Authority was allegedly regarded as a Habibie family concern.

Then there was the Bank Bali scandal. It seems that the bank paid over US$70 million as commission to a former vice-treasurer of the Golkar party in return for US$120 million in interbank loans frozen by Jakarta. The International Money Fund (IMF) and other major international lending agencies were angered by the corruption. This and the East Timor human rights breaches spelt doom for the Habibie regime. In both instances, international opinion went hard against Habibie.

The IMF and the World Bank demanded a thorough investigation of the Bali Bank fraud, and action taken against the perpetrators. But key figures involved, it was said, were Habibie's colleagues who were in his informal re-election team, optimistically designated "team success". People were seized with the conviction that large sums of money would be channelled into a vote-buying spree.

Megawati's opposition party, the PDI-P, accused several ministers, top politicians and high government officials of being implicated. Police and legal documents leaked to the press showed how blatant thievery involved people –

politicians, officials and businessmen – in the highest places. The least that could be said about the Bank Bali scandal was that Habibie had, in what he thought was rational management, handed over the utilisation of funds to his friends and relatives. But the scandal involved the siphoning of US$78 million, said to be for expenses for Golkar's bid to have Habibie re-elected as president.

Although the money was returned to Bank Bali, the bad odour remained. Whispers about Habibie's family involvement in the Nusantara Aircraft Industry and Batam's development, and the Bank Bali scandal, as well as other allegations, would inevitably link the president with the crony capitalism he was supposedly fighting.

All that, however, paled in comparison with the problems that erupted over East Timor, whish already had an interestingly chequered history. Starting as a receptor for various migratory tribes, Timor people were noted for their skill at iron-mongery and agriculture. Colonialism carved the island into two, the west grabbed by the Dutch, and the east falling into Portuguese hands. World War II had its sequel in the Dutch surrendering West Timor to the victorious Indonesian government. Portugal maintained its unsteady grasp of East Timor, although the country was racked by internal conflict. Indonesia favoured one of the sides in this internecine fight, and subsequently took over the governing of East Timor. The Front for the Liberation of East Timor carried on with guerilla warfare (Fretilin).

In Habibie's mind, that slice of Indonesia used too much of the entire country's resources. Moreover, international goodwill would be salvaged, and held-up loans would flow into Indonesia once more if Indonesia adopted a more liberal policy towards East Timor. But in the eyes of certain Indonesian military chiefs, East Timor was a challenge to retain within the Indonesian fold – by force, if necessary.

Habibie's analysis of the East Timor issue was the thinking of a rational scientist, not an astute politician. In the process, he enraged the military by allowing the East Timorese to vote themselves out of inclusion in Indonesia. The military feared that this would encourage separatist movements elsewhere in Indonesia. To the military, Indonesia as a unitary nation was a sacred fact. Habibie had pre-empted political or military intervention in what he had proposed about East Timor. He had ruled on giving the ballot to the East Timorese. They voted, unexpectedly but overwhelmingly, for secession. The Majelis Permusyawaratan Rakyat (MPR) or The People's Consultative Assembly decided to endorse the result of the ballot, despite the fact that the government had proceeded to carry on with the vote without the permission of the MPR. Apparently, Habibie's decision had prevailed.

By this time, the military establishment's patience with the new president was wearing thin. He had much earlier earned their jealousy when he received huge subventions from Suharto to pursue his ambitious plans to establish aircraft manufacturing in Indonesia. He had also bought second-hand naval vessels from east Germany, which the Indonesian military could not use. But more importantly, did not Habibie cut into the privileges of the military of making, and profiting from their own arms purchases?

Following the turmoil caused by East Timor's independence, Habibie agreed to the presence of a UN peace-keeping force there. Human Rights Watch hailed the president's decision as important and critical. Time was spent deciding on the conditions of UN intervention. Appeals were made to the Indonesian government to do all it could to prevent a bloodbath in the newly independent state.

The Indonesian generals, however, were actively fomenting destructive unrest, and instituting a pogrom against the East Timorese through militia trained by elements of the TNI. Half the population of East Timor was forcibly transmigrated to the western half of the island. That was the retribution for the large majority vote of nearly 80 per cent. When leaving East Timor, the Indonesian forces followed a scorched earth policy.

Thousands died as a result of East Timor's choice of independence from Indonesia. Habibie was blamed for granting East Timor independence, as well as for the United Nations' and foreign military intervention in East Timor. Habibie's decision to give the vote to East Timor and its disastrous consequences were universally execrated by the Indonesian people. The military who dominated Habibie's cabinet were, of course, ready to act against Habibie. When the time came, Wiranto, Minister for Defence and head of the armed forces, did not find this difficult, although the military was itself rent by conflict.

Despite Habibie's best intentions, the instability that marked Suharto's downfall continued with insignificant abatement. Intrigue marked all segments of the leadership. Habibie announced that he would call for new elections early, and would not wait until 2003, which would have been the constitutional limit to his rule. Political infighting intensified, as all pushed and shoved for favourable positions, in preparation for the electoral race. Demonstrations and protests continued. The military put down some of these.

While the Habibie regime could not bring about political stability, external confidence also fell. Economic aid from the International Monetary Fund was not forthcoming. In September 1999, a flurry of rumours had it that the military had staged a coup, taking over the government from Habibie. Perhaps no *armed* coup occurred.

Such a blatant step was unnecessary, and breached Javanese good manners. Habibie simply found he had to exercise his office under Wiranto's direct eye. During Habibie's 18-month rule, and in the subsequent regimes of Abdurrahman Wahid (Gus Dur) and Megawati Sukarnoputri, the ruling figures had to accept the ineluctable fact of the pervading and persistent power of the military, however much the TNI itself might be divided.

While Habibie's decision on East Timor was calamitous, there was, perhaps, a more basic reason for his losing ground. While the president showed an overweening self-confidence in interviews with journalists, Gus Dur, who would later emerge into greater political prominence, assessed him as one who did not understand the *rakyat*, the ordinary people, the people in the market-place.

A supremely ironic example of this was Habibie's temporary collusion with then cooperatives minister Adi Sasono. In the name of an allegedly Muslim-based concept of the People's Economy, Habibie suggested that Muslims fast twice a week in order to reduce consumption of rice. This would result in the saving of three million tons of rice per year. This would reduce completely Indonesia's dependence on rice imports. Even when Habibie departed from high-tech deliberations, the improbable application of scientific solutions remained his rationale.

Habibie himself seemed caught in the trap of his own inaccurate self-appraisal. In a statement accepting UN peacekeepers for East Timor, Habibie claimed that he was determined to strengthen democracy and the rule of law, to stabilise the economy and guarantee human rights. However, when Suharto had merely suggested Habibie as a presidential candidate, the rupiah's value plunged 20 per cent to an all-time low. When he did become president, business became depressed because of fears of Habibie's extravagant spending and his emulation of Suharto's corrupt practices.

There was every reason for someone like General Wiranto to keep a close eye on Habibie, whose fatal flaw (some Western commentators said) had been his inability to end the privileges of the military. This reflected the Alice-in-Wonderland outlook of those same commentators who could think that the power and privilege of the military could be curtailed, within a short time, in a single brief regime.

This was to view Indonesia from a totally clinical and rational viewpoint, and to ignore its history of struggle against colonialism and later against communism, in which the military played a *sine qua non* part, albeit it was bloody. Post-Habibie attempts to clip the military's wings evoked the same raising of hackles and restrained baring of fangs.

Still Habibie persevered in his, or his minders' political goal. Even as late as mid-October 1999, Golkar was still pushing Habibie as its candidate in the presidential election, scheduled to take place on the evening of October 20. Behind the Golkar effort was Akbar Tandjung, head of Golkar, and Speaker of Parliament's lower house of representatives. Akbar Tandjung was later jailed for corruption in 2002 but the sentence was overturned, and he was freed in time to contest the 2004 elections.

Judgement against Habibie was recorded almost immediately, namely in the late hours of October 19, after Habibie tried to defend his earlier accountability speech, against the critics of his apologia. His defence of his 16-month rule was rejected by a relatively small but convincing majority. Habibie's Western-trained mind had sought to present the justification of his regime on the rational grounds of his achievements. Habibie represented himself as practically being Indonesia's economic saviour. He boasted that he had planted the country firmly on the path to democracy. In the light of what he claimed he had been determined to do, from the beginning of his regime, perhaps the cards were stacked against him.

Habibie could be said to betray too much *yang* – the masculine, logical, cerebral principle; and not a *yang* balanced against the feminine *yin* principle of intuition and understanding of emotion and inward motivation. To put it another way, there was too much IQ in Habibie's outlook, and not enough EQ.

The military vote, impelled as much by group interests as nationalistic feelings, had very likely been the effective factor in repudiating Habibie's defence. But the narrow margin of his defeat – 322 for and 355 against – was perhaps the Javanese way of saving face for the Buginese, by saying yes, but definitely no. Habibie had to make way for a successor. He announced his withdrawal from the presidential contest on October 20, just hours before the presidential election was due to start. Akbar Tandjung had repudiated his original support for the president.

# CHAPTER 2

# GUS DUR SNEAKS IN

I N JUNE 1999, Megawati Sukarnoputri's PDI-P had won the highest number of votes to the Indonesian parliament, a little more than a third of those cast. But about five months later, she could not turn this favourable majority into a successful bid for the presidency. Even the military which was said to look favourably on her, decided to linger in their support for her. The blind Gus Dur ("She cannot talk, I cannot see") instead took over the seat.

One of the principal reasons Abdurrahman Wahid surged forward in the presidential race, was that Megawati's political coyness and reticence dismayed her followers. More importantly, these qualities did nothing to instil confidence and admiration for her in the minds of those in the Majelis Permusyawaratan Rakyat (MPR or People's Consultative Assembly) who were, constitutionally, the president-makers.

The system of election to the MPR gave the Jakarta-based elite an oligarchic thrust that a new-born Indonesian democracy, still in swaddling clothes, was not able to push aside. It was not necessarily conclusive that a candidate winning the most votes in the election to the House of Representatives (DPR) – like Megawati – would have the best chance of becoming president, the election of whom was the MPR's job.

In the event, a so-called central axis (*poros tengah*) of Muslim forces, already latent and quietly influenced by Amien Rais, and others including Wahid himself, emerged and dominated the MPR election results. On October 20, Habibie suddenly dropped out of the race, totally discouraged by the MPR's rejection of his apologia for his regime. Akbar Tandjung was himself involved in an uncertain flurry of candidates whose names came to the fore on Election Day itself.

But Akbar Tandjung and Amien Rais strayed diffidently away from their own nomination. An important realisation remained that there was no Muslim candidate to strive against the sole remaining figure of Megawati Sukarnoputri. At that time also, the Muslim establishment was querulous over the possibility of a woman becoming president.

Such prejudice lay deep in the public psyche. Such an underlying cultural bias would remain and arise again later at a moment of crisis during Megawati's regime. But just when it looked as if Megawati's hope of becoming president would be realised, Muslim activist Yusril Ihza Mahendra offered his candidacy. Yusril Ihza Mahendra from the Crescent Star Party soon realised, just before the balloting, that Abdurrahman Wahid had made a last-minute decision to contest also. Wahid had previously promised to support Megawati's aspiration to be president. Gus Dur, as Wahid was popularly known, claimed that he wanted to make the contest more democratic. Megawati's return, in default of competition, would seem a poor democratic outcome.

However, it was highly likely that Gus Dur, in private, possibly an anti-feminist himself, doubted whether Megawati had the political wisdom to take the first place in leading the country out of the current tumult. She herself was riding on the crest of hysterical popular acclaim. Although Megawati herself displayed a coy political outlook, Gus Dur was wary of the PDI-P masses, mobilised with an undoubted view to coerce political outcomes.

In a sudden one-hour drama, the other contender in the presidential race – Yusril Ihza Mahendra – who had opted in, swiftly opted out. The behind-the-scenes manoeuvring was betrayed by the effusive congratulations showered on Mahendra on his withdrawal, as opposed to the consternation the announcement of his candidacy at first brought. In fact, so enthusiastic was the thanksgiving that the embarrassed man had to brush it off with some show of annoyance.

What eventually happened on the fateful night of October 20 was that a coalition of a newly constructed yet apparently highly effective axis of Muslim forces, together with military and Golkar interests, gave the presidency to Gus Dur with a convincing 373 votes as against Megawati's 313. All hell broke loose. Thousands of sobbing, frustrated supporters of Megawati, tried to storm the People's Assembly, but police succeeded in holding them back. There were casualties on both sides, some caused by a couple of mysterious bomb blasts. It was clear that no political calculations at the top could afford to leave out Megawati. She was, for the time, the iconic inheritor of the force of the Sukarno myth. She had won more than a third of the popular vote. If *vox populi* counted for anything, her majority represented a formidable tigerish roar.

The next day on October 21, Megawati was elected vice-president. In her characteristic way, she seemed at first reluctant to contest for the vice-presidency. She feared a similar loss of face that her defeat the night before had produced.

But the (staged) withdrawal from the vice-presidential race of General Wiranto and Akbar Tandjung left only one contender – Hamzah Haz – an important figure in the Muhammadiyah, the leader of Muslim party PPP and Deputy Speaker of Parliament. Megawati felt that her bruised self-confidence could take this candidate on. Megawati won, and her constituency was appeased. Gus Dur and Megawati on first appearance seemed an impressive tandem.

Two of Megawati's ablest and best-qualified supporters were immediately included in Gus Dur's cabinet. Kwik Kian Gie, regarded as Megawati's number two, became Coordinating Minister for the Economy, Finance and Industry PDI-P treasurer Laksamana Sukardi was appointed Minister in Charge of Investment. Kwik, of Chinese descent, was a brilliant economist with a clean reputation.

Habibie had offered him a position as chairman of Indonesia's investment coordinating board which Kwik had turned down. He explained frankly that, with Indonesia's economy in such a woeful condition, he would have had to clown it out with barefaced lies. However, he appeared willing to try his hand in Gus Dur's cabinet, accepting a graver responsibility in worse economic conditions.

Kwik's willingness to go along with Gus Dur must have been due to his unfailing loyal to Megawati. He had stood by her during the trying days when Suharto's cohorts succeeded in ousting Megawati from her position as head of the PDI-P. He helped her form the PDI-P– the Indonesian Democratic Party – Struggle. Kwik's CV listed him as being head of a succession of several business concerns in Indonesia, Holland and Zanzibar (presumably for spices for the *kretek* cigarettes).

Sukardi was an engineer turned banker. He had won the title Banker of the Year in 1992. He attempted to lead a reform movement in the banking and financial sector. Sukardi believed that rapid democratisation was the key to stability and economic recovery.

As in the case of Habibie's cabinet, the military occupied key positions in Gus Dur's cabinet. But a civilian, Yuwono Sudarsono, became Defence Minister, for the first time, it seems, in Indonesia's history. Sudarsono, former university dean, had been Habibie's education minister. General Wiranto, former defence minister, became Coordinating Minister for Political and Security Affairs. He retained his position as armed forces chief.

Gus Dur called his a cabinet of national unity. He had put into this Pandora's box, representations from a wide variety of interests. Pressure had come from influential figures – Megawati, Wiranto, Amien Rais and Akbar Tandjung, to name perhaps an important few. But critics raised doubts about the character of the cabinet members. Some of the military appointees, it appeared, had been involved in Suharto's regime of corruption, collusion and nepotism (KKN). There were even accusations against Wiranto for having been involved in human rights breaches.

Although Gus Dur spoke at first of his "rainbow" cabinet, he knew all the time that what had been foisted on him by various interested parties was a "*rojak*" (a local salad) plate. Inasmuch as Gus Dur was, at first inwardly, then manifestly, unhappy with the newly formed cabinet, his persistent rival Amien

Rais was chuckling with satisfaction.

Amien Rais had actually succeeded in insinuating over half a dozen of his protegees in an antagonist's cabinet. He had been prominent in manoeuvring the central organisation of Muslim forces towards voting Gus Dur into office. But for Gus Dur, having Rais' fifth column in his cabinet was an unpleasant dilemma.

# CHAPTER 3

# GUS DUR TRAVELS

ABDURRAHMAN Wahid, soon after he became president, began a series of visits to other countries, punctuated by domestic political action when he returned. The first thing the president did after he had settled the first, original composition of his cabinet was to make a flying visit to eight Asean countries.

In Singapore, Gus Dur blandly recounted how he felt Singapore was like a second home to him. He claimed he had always looked upon his highly prosperous neighbour in a fraternal light. He assured Indonesian businessmen that he would make the legal and economic circumstances more conducive for the return of their expatriated capital.

Gus Dur promised in Singapore to clean up his government, and provide a guarantee of legal security. Indonesian-Chinese businessmen, who had allegedly parked billions in Singapore, expressed their optimism over the new Indonesian president's assurance. Several said they believed money would flow back to Indonesia again. In his early days, Gus Dur was sanguine. And he inspired his hearers with optimism.

In Cambodia, Gus Dur told of how one of his maternal ancestors had been a princess of ethnic Chinese descent from Champa. To a person who has enjoyed some familiarity with Indonesia, and is acquainted with Javanese legends, such reminiscences of Gus Dur's evoke a rich tradition. There are many stories of *puteri Cina* (Chinese princesses) who had been sent to Java to marry Javanese royalty. They are reflected in carvings, paintings and other artistic representations too.

Gus Dur was manifesting a fine, sensitive cultural outlook that sought conciliation rather than an emphasis on the individual.

In Cambodia, Gus Dur shrugged off urgent news about Aceh. Cries for independence from the province had taken on a more insistent note. As the situation grew critical, Gus Dur said he did not mind if Aceh wanted a referendum over its independence. If he meant that there were means to solve the Aceh problem, he did not palliate anxiety in Jakarta by saying how it could be done.

In Manila, the Indonesian president incidentally referred to Sukarno's close friendship with Daud Beureuh – an Acehnese leader (indeed "father of the Acehnese people") who was commander of Darul Islam, a militant Islamic organisation. Perhaps Gus Dur was implying that an Indonesian leader could relate to militant Islam, under certain circumstances. Daud Beureuh had voiced forthcoming sentiments of a more tolerant Islam – after the establishment of an Islamic regime.

Sukarno, the father of vice-president Megawati Sukarnoputri, had apparently given Daud Beureuh hope for the establishment of an Islamic state. When this did not come about, the Acehnese "lion" – reputed to be equal in eloquence to Sukarno – turned against the latter.

Against a background of querulous, opportunistic voices raised back home as to what the president was doing abroad at a time like this, Gus Dur remained unfazed. He even spoke of his expectation that there would be a meeting between him and Hasan de Tiro, the self-exiled chief of the Acehnese rebel fighters. Was Wahid imagining a repeat of the Sukarno scenario with Daud Beureuh? De Tiro promptly dashed such hopes. Gus Dur's mystifying pronouncements, if they did not infuriate, certainly caused blood pressures to rise in Jakarta.

Next came the off and on reports during Gus Dur's Asean trip about his impending trip to the United States to meet President Bill Clinton. Gus Dur had scarcely returned to Jakarta when he took off on November 11 for the US. It had been only three weeks since he was returned as president that the suspicion started to grow that this new leader was going to be peripatetic. As a sort of soother, Gus Dur's aides stressed that the president was travelling to the US on a commercial flight, thus saving the government coffers a sum of nearly US$150,000. They were keen to make a point of Gus Dur's willingness to economise, even if it was a small matter. It is important to note that, despite the American president's busy schedule, he was tabled to meet the Indonesian leader. As for Abdurrahman Wahid, in the current scheme of *his* priorities, the US meeting was more urgent than events unfolding in Aceh.

On Gus Dur's American visit, two former US ambassadors to Indonesia were still serving as Indonesia watchers. It was reported that US investors shared former envoy Ed Master's sanguine outlook brought about by the early encounter between the heads of state. All the same, the Americans were waiting hopefully for Gus Dur's specific acts to address financial and judicial reforms. Paul Wolfowitz, former US ambassador to Indonesia, and at that time an inhabitant of Johns Hopkins University, commented that it was significant that Clinton had agreed, with little warning, to fit in a meeting with Gus Dur into his schedule. Wolfowitz interpreted Clinton's decision as a (positive) signal to investors.

The visit also gave Gus Dur and his attending officials an encounter with International Monetary Fund and World Bank representatives. More essentially, Clinton said the right thing when he stated that it was important for Indonesia to preserve its territorial integrity. Clinton offered to help Gus Dur to face this difficult challenge. The US president suggested support for Wahid's decision to further democracy. Gus Dur also thanked Clinton for supporting inter faith dialogue.

This held an oblique reference to Gus Dur's plan to ease relations with Israel in the economic sector. Gus Dur, with his characteristic inclusivism, spoke about getting together the "three Abrahamic traditions" – Islam, Judaism and Christianity. In Utah, Gus Dur reportedly stayed at the residence of Mormon leader, Hal Jensen.

When Wahid returned to Indonesia, he somehow got Hamzah Haz to resign from his cabinet post of Coordinating Minister for People's Welfare. Hamzah Haz was the former Muhammadiyah chief. The reason Hamzah gave for his resignation was his difference of opinion with the president over relations with Israel. Apparently Gus Dur did not mind some indirect business links with Israel but Hamzah declared his opposition to such a move.

At the same time, Hamzah was reportedly called to the Attorney-General's office in connection with some investigation into alleged corruption. The cabinet which reflected the varied and conflicting interests of nationalists, Muslim axis, Golkar and the military would be bound to be affected by political rivalries. Indeed one philosophy of politics which had been enunciated by no other than Hamzah Haz was that there was no cooperation or even opposition that was permanent. There was only change.

Less than a week after he returned from his US-Japan tour, the president set off for the Middle East. He was scheduled to meet Palestinian leader Yasser Arafat in Jordan, within a framework of visits to Jordan, Kuwait and Qatar, from November 22-25. In the midst of this trip, Gus Dur announced that the decision to open trade relations with Israel had been put off.

But Gus Dur could not release the bit once he had it between his teeth. Adapting his tack, he said that trade contacts with Israel would be useful for Indonesia to play a role in the Palestinian peace process. More importantly there would be economic dividends for Indonesia from his latest schedule, in terms of attracting foreign investments from Arab countries.

From Kuwait, Qatar and Amman, Gus Dur urged Indonesian entrepreneurs to take advantage of the markets in the Gulf States. Although their capita income was high, Indonesian businessmen had treated such markets lightly, while showing more interest in the United States and Japan.

Gus Dur also managed to get mileage for the Aceh problem in his Middle East visit. As one Muslim country to another, Qatar appealed to Aceh not to break away from Indonesia, offering the province assistance with its development.

Thus Gus Dur, through his many visits abroad, was using a form of long-distance governance, via diplomatic means. Perhaps he hoped that (a) pressure from an economic power from the West (the US and Bill Clinton) for Indonesia to remain one, and (b) added appeals from Muslim players in the Middle East for unhappy elements in Indonesia not to break away, would help him in his domestic efforts.

In Jordan, Gus Dur showed he was aware of the continued clamour on the part of Indonesia's military for martial law to be imposed in Aceh. He rejected this military option out of hand. He also repeated his definition of the parameters for a referendum on Aceh. It would not be about independence but on whether Aceh wanted rule according to Islamic law. The president wanted to show how he continued to monitor his domestic politics, and that he could hold the reins even when he was abroad.

Gus Dur stoutly refused to be persuaded by the exhortations of the military. By offering Aceh the option of Syariah rule, he was (as some ancestral strategists on Gus Dur's Chinese side might say) taking out some of the fire that had been heating up the cauldron of Acehnese hatred. By showing that he was trying to help the Acehnese economically, through his discussions in the Middle East, he hoped he would douse the fire further. At the same time, Gus Dur was also trying to tame his own Muslim revanchists at home by strengthening his ties with Muslim friendlies abroad and enlisting their sympathy.

On Gus Dur's return on November 26, he announced the resignation of Coordinating Minister Hamzah Haz. The withdrawal of a cabinet minister so soon after he had been appointed of course triggered interested speculation. Hamzah's explanation that as head of the PPP party, he was too involved with his responsibilities, could not hold much water. Why had he not said so earlier?

In truth, Hamzah Haz and Gus Dur had been mutual protagonists for some time. Hamzah had once been in Nadlatul Ulama but entertained a different political standpoint from Gus Dur. Hamzah Haz left the Nadlatul Ulama when intolerable differences arose, to rest his fortune with the PPP. It was then that Gus Dur formed the National Awakening Party (PKB). It is said that the latest clash between the two politicians occurred when Hamzah Haz lost the vice-presidential election (to be Gus Dur's vice-president!) against Megawati Sukarnoputri who was staunchly supported by Gus Dur.

Wahid must have long sensed Hamzah Haz's potential for political acrobatics. This was to be amply shown in Megawati's regime that followed the fall of Gus Dur in 2001. But for the present, it was Gus Dur who decided to get rid of what could be, or maybe already was, a thorn in his flesh. He did this by whispering about Hamzah's alleged involvement in corruption.

Hamzah retaliated by stressing his Islamic prescription. He said he could not tolerate Abdurrahman Wahid's dallying with possible relations with Israel. This was cunning, and indicated that the agile politician from Pontianak, in Indonesian Borneo, still very much entertained ambitions of a high order, which he hoped to achieve by riding on the chariot of Islam.

Meanwhile, Gus Dur continued his programme of overseas visits. An interesting aside to Gus Dur's tours abroad was a one-off reverse visit. This was the significant arrival in Jakarta of Japan's prime minister, Keizo Obuchi, for discussions with economic officials and the Indonesian president. Many expectations were adduced for Obuchi's visit. Japan intended to send experts to advise Indonesia on small and medium industries. An agreement was hopefully in the offing to induce Japanese investment in Indonesiaa.

Apparently, Obuchi had been impressed by Gus Dur's friendliness. The Japanese premier was on his way to attend the Asean Conference. The importance that he gave to Indonesia was interesting in that he decided to make a two-day stopover in Jakarta, although he would be seeing Gus Dur in Manila anyway.

Obuchi's visit highlighted the fact that Gus Dur would himself be resuming his overseas trips, this time to Asean's informal summit at Manila and then for an official visit to China. Ominous murmurings were heard in Jakarta that Gus Dur seemed to assess external politics as much more important than the Aceh crisis. Gus Dur was also beginning to erode relations with the military by declaring that a state of military emergency, which the military wanted in Aceh, was out of the question.

Leaving such explosive differences behind him in Jakarta, Gus Dur went to Manila and briefed his Asean colleagues and the three East Asian leaders of China, Japan and South Korea on Aceh. As a result, Singapore leader Goh Chok Tong proposed that Asean craft a statement supporting Indonesia's territorial integrity and sovereignty. It was obvious that such conditions would be of consequence to Asean also. In this circumstance, the three East Asian countries voiced their assent.

It was becoming clear that the Indonesian president hoped that his cool yet nimble strategy of travel to muster support, instead of listening to what he thought were panicky voices at home, would pay dividends towards a solution in Aceh. Reviewing such a stance, it was Gus Dur's energetic round after round of visits that secured understanding and sympathy expressed by the United States – the world's most powerful country; selected Arab countries'– representing Islamic opinion; Japan – significant for Indonesia's economic recovery; and Asean states – Indonesia's near neighbours.

The president had, within a short space of a month, visited 13 countries. He followed this with his first official, visit to China. A large contingent of officials and about 90 businessmen and entrepreneurs accompanied him. Gus Dur asked the Chinese side not to let perceptions that Indonesia discriminated against the Chinese affect mutual relations. He was regretful but not defensive about this. He pointed out that among the Chinese community were those whose behaviour provoked negative reactions. One decision over which there was immediate agreement was that the Bank of China should open a branch in Indonesia.

Perhaps the declaration most significant for amiable Sino-Indonesian accord, when Gus Dur was in China, was his determination to ensure equal oportunities for Chinese and those of Chinese ethnic origin with the so-called *pribumis*. He also promised to revoke restrictions on the development of Chinese culture, including the use of Chinese characters outside Chinese establishments. He spoke of developing a better understanding of Chinese culture, including encouraging the study of Mandarin and Confucianism.

The Muslim social organisation, Muhammadiyah, on Gus Dur's return from China, coincidentally resolved to urge the government to recognise the existence of Confucianism in Indonesia, and make such a provision legal. Thus Gus Dur's policy of liberalising attitudes towards things Chinese would not find opposition from Muslim organisations, as Nadlatul Ulama together with Muhammadiyah would represent the bulk of Muslims both in urban and country areas.

In fact, Chinese New Year, or Imlek, was raised from the status of an optional holiday (during Gus Dur's time) to that of a public, or national, holiday when Megawati Sukarnoputri came into power. Obviously, there was popular support for such an understanding of, and favour towards, this aspect of Chinese cultural expression.

# CHAPTER 4

# GUS DUR'S PROBLEMS WITH THE MILITARY

FROM a political observer's viewpoint, Gus Dur's fifteen-day fifth overseas schedule, from January 30 to February 13, must have been the most suspenseful. It was during his travels to Europe, India and South Korea that Gus Dur announced that General Wiranto, senior minister in charge of security and politics, should resign. Wiranto had been named responsible for human rights abuses during his tenure as armed forces chief. From almost every capital or city he visited – London, Davos in Switzerland, Belgium, Germany (on television in Berlin), Rome and even the Vatican – Gus Dur sent the same message through statements to the media: Wiranto should resign.

Saying Wiranto was his friend, and he would find a way to pardon the general if he admitted his responsibility, Gus Dur even revealed how Wiranto had, in fact, warned him of a possible assassination attempt against the president and vice-president of Indonesia.

Wiranto resisted the calls from afar for him to give up his cabinet post. He said this would appear as admitting his culpability. He was ready to accept responsibility, but needed to explain the circumstances surrounding the devastation that took place in East Timor after it was granted independence. Wiranto claimed he took no part at all in the East Timor excesses. Indeed, he even brokered a peace accord there. He would therefore wait until Gus Dur returned from overseas. But the president continued his long-distance appeals. Wiranto's delay in announcing his resignation was damaging Indonesia's immediate chances of attracting foreign investment. A group of generals intended to see Wiranto to persuade him to step down. On television, Wiranto put up a brave front, but his initial jaunty demeanour seemed to wear thin towards the end of Gus Dur's foreign tour.

Meanwhile, seemingly unfazed by his long-distance political exercise with an erstwhile and possibly still powerful general, Gus Dur continued his journey to New Delhi. Here he reaffirmed Indonesia's desire to join in strategic association with Asian giants India and China. With his usual outlook, he spoke of how much Indonesian culture owed to India, even quoting the high percentage of words in the Javanese, indeed even Indonesian, language which came from Sanskrit.

He then spent the last few days of his schedule travelling to South Korea. Here he intended to make a valiant attempt to persuade the South Koreans to resurrect their joint car industrial project with Indonesia, which had commenced towards the end of the Suharto regime. Gus Dur also made a brief mention of the possibility of cooperation with Malaysia in car manufacturing, to widen the market. However, this was very likely a typical Gus Dur strategy of flying a balloon to test the atmosphere.

From New Delhi and Seoul, Gus Dur continued his appeal to Wiranto to resign. However, immediately on his return from his fifteen-day tour, the media reported that President Abdurrahman Wahid had decided to defer his decision to seek Wiranto's resignation. Then in a *volte face*, proclaimed in a surprising dawn media announcement on Monday, February 14, 2000, it was reported that on Sunday night, Gus Dur had decided to declare Wiranto – who had been coordinating minister for political affairs and security – non-active.

Abdurrahman Wahid's distant and close encounters with Wiranto reflected his tentative and unsure attempts to whittle down the power of the military. The designation of the armed forces had been changed from ABRI to TNI (Tentara Nasional Indonesia or Indonesian National Army). Such a change had been foreseen since 1988. The current Indonesian president, Dr Yudhoyono, had been one of its authors and was put in charge of territorial affairs which, in fact, continued to oversee the spread of army control.

It has been argued that the only really substantive change in the name of the Indonesian armed forces was that the qualifier "National" had been added. ABRI had a dual function – a military as well as a socio-political one. *"ABRI masok desa"* was a popular cry meaning "the armed forces enter the villages", indicating ABRI's extent of responsibility and control. Gus Dur hoped that ABRI's successor, TNI, would gradually concentrate on its military functions and develop itself professionally, while leaving politics to civilians. Gus Dur's feelings about the military's role was not an uncommon one, and not unpopular from a civic outlook. But it was naturally unpopular with most of the military – and certainly with its powerful personages.

The military was not only involved in politics through a dual function (*dwi-fungsi*), in which it had established parallel governance with the civil administration, it was also involved in the economy. Military units had formed business cooperatives or corporations. The revenue from such business bodies was supposed to augment the poor allocation of resources from official coffers. Military-owned enterprises eventually melded into the business and industrial conglomerates of the Suharto family and their cronies, including privileged major Chinese entrepreneurs.

Thus the military only made grudging concessions to the democratisation process. They agreed to reduce their representation in parliament in stages marked by each presidential election. But they held out, even bitterly, against one who strenuously criticised the military for their hold on political power and continued corruption. Reformist Letjen (Lt-General) Agus Wirahadikusumah brought odium on himself and the wrath of powerful military chiefs for his publicly stated views on *reformasi* as it involved the military.

Agus Wirahadikusumah (Agus WK) scorned *dwi-fungsi*. He proposed the reduction in numbers and even abolition of regional and district military commands. He thought the *Babinsa* quite superfluous. The *Babinsa* were non-commissioned military personnel posted to villages, and affiliated with the civilian administration. *Dwi-fungsi* represented level by level structures occupied by the military, parallel to a civilian framework. Agus WK seemed to think that the military "administrative and control" structures were cannibalising on the civil administration.

Agus WK saw such structures as an illegitimate network supporting the corruption of those who, even in military school, nurtured ambitions of attaining high civilian positions of regent, governor and minister. The farming out of commands, major or petty, brought magnificent opportunities of economic tribute to gratified officers. The top echelon in the military dismissed Agus WK's ideas as idealistic and his behaviour as not in keeping with military ethics.

It was only about four months since Gus Dur had come to power, and now he had become entangled with an unpopular reformist and his small group of followers. Obviously, Gus Dur recognised the almost insurmountable difficulty he faced in his task of leading Indonesia on the path to reform and democratisation. The military was intent on blocking the way. Their economic interests were being threatened. Since such interests had a territorial spread it was to the military's benefit to retain the territorial commands.

Maluku was a prime example of upheavals manipulated by the military to show their desire to exercise control in the regions. They did this through Muslim militia and other proxies. Inevitably, as in pre-communist China, in *zaibatsu* (corporate bodies of) Japan, in pre-PAP Singapore, big business in Indonesia became joined to underworld activities.

Large numbers of Golkar's Pancasila Youth joined other groups of political gangsters, assault and battery brigades and provocateurs. Many of these received training under the auspices of expert, tough, ruthless military figures, some still in active service. Many of these eager novices were drafted into so-called militia units. Some of the military thus produced their own thugs to collude with the political variety.

Gus Dur came into conflict with these strong-arm boys. During *Orde*

*Baru* time Suharto could be visualised breathing his avuncular spirit over these volunteers. Eminent among these was one who was even a neighbour of Gus Dur. Yorrys Rawehai, of part Chinese and part-Papuan ancestry, loved Suharto like a son towards his father, and the old despot responded like a godfather. With the military as superstructure, such was the insidious underground distribution of power that Gus Dur knew he had inherited. He could do nothing except hint that he knew the game.

Then along came Agus Wirahadikusumah. In truth, this general was a military thinker far ahead of his time. Even his superiors thought so. But they feared his insistence on applying his radical reformist ideas. He opposed the extension of the *Kodam* (military regions) structure. He criticised *dwi-fungsi* mercilessly, because it detracted from the military's professionalism. The military's dominance had to be diminished, step by step he agreed, for Indonesia to evolve into a democracy. He wanted to abolish the TNI's territorial functions, because it contradicted autonomy in the provinces.

Gus Dur embraced Agus Wirahadikusumah like a brother. He promoted him, making him commander of Kostrad (strategic land forces) in March 2000. Four months later Agus WK, whose father had been vice-president to Suharto, was plucked from Kostrad. Those officers in sympathy with him were transferred from their current posts.

It was suggested that Agus WK's fall from grace resulted from his uncovering of a financial scandal in the Yayasan Dharma Putra, a company owned by Kostrad. It was General Wiranto, whom Gus Dur had rendered "non-active" with Agus WK's help, that agitated for Agus' dismissal. Top TNI brass also lobbied vice-president Megawati Sukarnoputri for action against Agus. Gus Dur felt the pressure too much to withstand, and acceded to the persuasions around him. Megawati's hearkening to the military would obviously make her its favourite.

But Gus Dur did not give up over Agus WK. He tried to place his nominee as army chief of staff, when the job was about to fall vacant. Again, TNI senior officers and Megawati pressured Gus Dur, and told him that a number of generals would request for early retirement if the president proceeded with his intention. And so Letjen Endriartono Sutarto became army and later TNI chief. Gus Dur had miscalculated and led the military ultimately to back Megawati. About a year following, to everybody's deep shock and dismay, Agus Wirahadikusumah died suddenly of a heart attack.

Gus Dur's contest with the military consisted, as already seen, of hit-and-run tactics. His distant and close skirmishes with Wiranto illustrated this. To the military Gus Dur was, willy-nilly, a spoiler. It was highly likely that the military had expected Megawati to become president in October 1999. Then Wiranto would have been her vice-president, a position of strategic influence.

Unfortunately for this plan, Abdurrahman Wahid rode in on the back of politically persuaded Muslim voters. Additional persuasion from Letjen

Tyasno Sudarto and Wiranto strengthened Megawati's assent to contest against Hamzah Haz for the vice-president's post. Because of Megawati's political dominance as chief of PDI-P, *she* had to be vice-president. But because of the support of Tyasno Sudarto and Wiranto, Megawati's relations with the military would be affected favourably.

The military consented to the decision that all military officers holding high civilian posts had to resign their commissions. Edi Sudradjat contested whether the president should also be supreme commander of the armed forces. It had been a sanctimonious mantra that the members of the Indonesian armed forces took an oath of loyalty to the president as their overall chief. Gus Dur, indignant over Sudradjat's query, promptly asked armed forces chief Widodo to sack Sudradjat.

Sudradjat, after retirement, continued to express his utter lack of confidence in Gus Dur. But the military itself was, organisation-wise, in disorder. Without the strong control exercised by Suharto or Benny Murdani, rivalry between camps and individuals within the TNI surfaced. Officers spent much time planning their career paths, without a thought for problems faced by the ordinary soldier. Gus Dur thought he might take advantage of such weaknesses. But at critical junctures, the top command closed ranks against Gus Dur.

In Gus Dur's time, Agus Widjojo became prominent in the public eye, until he reached the rank of Letjen. His was a voice of moderation that Gus Dur should have paid more attention to. Shortly after Gus Dur was forced to step down in 2001, Letjen Agus Widjojo became Deputy Speaker in the MPR. In June 2001, Agus rejected a call for the military to receive human rights training. He firmly thought that this would create confusion in the minds of his fighting men. Later, he enunciated the principle he wanted to start from: namely, that the TNI command understood command and responsibility. Michael Leifer of the London School of Economics and Political Science even raised the fear of a military coup. However, the TNI was weakened by divisions and discord, and could not mount an operation to seize power and establish itself as a paramount authority. In fact, the TNI was under attack from many quarters. Its generals were being accused of human rights violations, and a local examining body had been set up to investigate the culpability of certain figures, including General Wiranto. Nevertheless, the TNI had the means to look after its own.

It was reported that at the time Wiranto was called in for questioning, a group of hard-core Islamicists, members of the Front for the Defence of Islam (Front Pembela Islam or FPI), broke into the office where the proceedings were being held. Those present were asked to pray for the generals under investigation, for they were "our generals, our leaders". When Wiranto was sarcastically asked if the TNI had turned Islamic, Wiranto replied that the incident was a spontaneous one.

Nobody believed in the spontaneity of the demonstrations. The intruders were dressed uniformly in white. And armed with spears and machetes. Before the investigation into the generals' behaviour, the FPI did not show any interest in the investigatory commission's activities. But at the generals "trials", the FPI suddenly appeared and demanded that the commission be dissolved. It was noted that among the authors of the FPI were staunch friends of Wiranto like Djadja Suparman and Fachrul Razi.

Tough as the FPI seemed to be, there was one occasion when the organisation made itself look clownish. The awkward situation arose when a certain Brigjen Tono Suratman was called to appear before the National Enquiry Commission on human rights. The Brigjen entered followed by a group of FPI adherents who showed themselves prepared to stand by Tono Suratman througout the period of his interrogation.

The loyal members of the Front for the Defence of Islam were therefore thrown into some confusion when, after diligently following the interrogation, they suddenly became aware that Tono Suratman was a Roman Catholic whose Christian name was Franciscus Xaverius. It was an embarassing situation, and the FPI group meekly left the Enquiry Commission's premises.

One rarely looks for humorous anecdotes – and finds them – in a complex political environment such as Indonesia's. The Suratman case was unique in that respect. Religion was generally manipulated to achieve various ends, with far more serious consequences. Muslim radical militia were summoned to protect generals under threat of prosecution; *jihad* warriors, to strike awe and terror when a threat to Indonesia's unity was imagined as in Maluku, or to commit mayhem, as in the burning of the Christian seminary, Doulos, in Jakarta; or to "cleanse" establishments in Jogjakarta and to frighten Americans.

The principal puppeteers could be various figures, although the temptation was to point the finger at shadowy personalities associated with the Suharto family, who were prominent members of the former military and business elite. Gus Dur knew who these hidden evil hands were. He could not name them, because they would inevitably demand irrefutable evidence.

The Suharto clan had no reason to love Gus Dur. Suharto himself asserted that the way he had chosen to govern Indonesia was the best way. In his mind, one had to continue running the country his way. Suharto's choice of Habibie to succeed him was no doubt influenced by the thought that the *Orde Baru* system might be restored. But Habibie's *hubris* brought about a succeeding regime to replace his.

While Habibie did not take up legal charges against Suharto, Abdurrahman Wahid began rigorous action. Gus Dur promised a pardon for Suharto, provided that the former despot would come clean over the $150 million he was accused of embezzling. Suharto's informal successors to the previous New Order regime began to loathe Gus Dur's temerity.

In any case, total confusion prevailed wherever rogue elements of the TNI wanted it to. This would be seen more clearly later when the confusion spread from Maluku into neighbouring Sulawesi, and threatened further to extend into West Irian and even to Aceh during the following Megawati regime. The means used was the Laskar Jihad, Islamic military elements under the command of Ja'far Umar Thalib, still an active agent of the Indonesian National Army.

Such subversive activities were intended to diminish the stature of the president, and jeer at the civil administration. Already, within months of the start of Gus Dur's regime, those who had supported him initially were hatching plans to bring him down. Such movements appeared coordinated and capable of spontaneity. Massive demonstrations to protest against the killings of Muslims in Maluku took place at Monas, the site of the National Monument, in Jakarta. Such manifestations also called for holy war. Gus Dur declared that such calls were unconstitutional. The organisers declared that *jihad* did not necessarily mean armed action. Amien Rais hurried to assure Gus Dur that he had the former's support until the constitutional end of Gus Dur's rule.

Not only was political guerilla sniping added to the chaos in Maluku, the specific nexus between evil intention and violent action could also be occasionally discerned. Singapore's prime minister at the time, Goh Chok Tong, during a brief visit to Indonesia, presented Gus Dur with a S$1.5 billion package of proposals and cooperation in tourism. Scarcely had the Singapore leader returned to Singapore when rioting erupted in Bintan in the Riau Archipelago, and virtually on Singapore's doorstep, where Singapore finance had joined Indonesian money in putting up rapidly developing industrial investments and tourist projects. Additionally, agitators went to work in Lombok, an island next to Indonesian tourist paradise Bali, arousing Muslims on the island, who had previously lived in harmony with Christians, to attack Christians and burn their churches. Chinese establishments soon also became the targets of mob fury. Bali itself, for the time, appeared to have been spared, because the majority of the population was Hindu.

But threatening leaflets appeared in the popular tourist location, and Chinese houses and business premises were daubed with lettering to show which were destined for burning. Both venues of rioting so separated by distance as Bintan and Lombok were targeted for disturbance to cock a snook at those who thought that they would help Indonesia with a tourism and industrial recovery.

Abdurrahman Wahid earned unpopularity for himself when he resorted to rumour-mongering to discomfit his foes. Wiranto was obviously foremost among those who were against Gus Dur. But the general had to smile and smile and be a villain. Meanwhile, Gus Dur embarked on a string of allegations. He said there was a plot to assassinate him. A secret meeting of generals had taken place in Jakarta. Gus Dur even named the location – Laotze Street (Jalan

Laotze). Wahid also claimed that a ceasefire agreement had been reached with Acehnese rebel leaders, which the Acehnese promptly denied.

The media also carried a report that, at a mid-March 2000 TV dialogue session, entitled "A cup of coffee", Gus Dur claimed that one of his senior military commanders would (try to) dismantle his leadership. Gus Dur had chosen Idul Adha (Hari Raya Haji) to time another of his off-hand deliveries. He said that there was one mischievous general among his eleven territorial commanders.

Parliamentary dignitaries and Gus Dur's opposition critics accused him of making wild allegations. They concluded that these had been whisperings in his ear. They sought explanation from Wahid's aides, even from his daughter Yenny, who was invariably seen at her father's side. But Gus Dur was perhaps beating the bush to frighten the snake.

There had actually been a meeting at Jalan Laotze. It seems it was a gathering of rent-a-gang organizers ready to carry banners at any rally. It was alleged that the general behind it all, whether he was really present at the meeting or not, was Djadja Suparman, Kostrad chief, who had the Front for the Defence of Islam at his beck and call. He could be firmly placed in Wiranto's camp. The mass rally did not materialise.

But there was little doubt that staunch supporters of the Suharto establishment tried, even in the early days of Gus Dur's rule, to organise unrest through hired demonstrators to destabilise his regime. The high-level henchmen of Suharto were in close relations with the military.

Gus Dur's behaviour towards the military spelt out his intention to make it subordinate to the civil authority. That was the course of *reformasi*, the course of democratisation. But that was far easier said than done. Moreover, Gus Dur had to be careful not to be too precipitate in this intention.

The military had ruled the roost for three decades. Suharto himself had been a five-star general. Strong elements of the military hankered after the good old days. Gus Dur could not, and neither was it his intention, to humiliate the military. And he held before the military that they were ultimately defenders of the nation's integrity.

Gus Dur had to allow the civil authority a certain position when dealing with those elements of the military against whom charges of human rights offences had been made. He therefore tried to follow a good-guy, bad-guy policy. He made himself look as conciliatory as possible, while he allowed the attorney-general to push the no-nonsense legalistic line. This technique appeared to have been followed in the case of Gus Dur's (secret, later to be revealed) negotiations with the Suharto family for the retrieval of its wealth. Gus Dur talked of pardon, while attorney-general Marzuki Darusman laid down the law. Such ducking and weaving ultimately caused Gus Dur to be regarded as unstable and untrustworthy.

Critics accused Gus Dur of making impetuous and irresponsible remarks. Later, after his ouster, he charged that in the 1999 parliamentary elections, only 60 per cent of the votes had been counted by the election commission when President Habibie declared the winners. Gus Dur was trying to present the holders of DPR seats during his time as being unconstitutionally returned. He was thus trying to dismiss parliament before the MPR voted him out of office on July 22, 2001.

Such was the larger canvas against which he had asked the Supreme Court to judge whether he was violating the constitution or not in trying to disband parliament. The question also was whether the military elements who refused to obey Gus Dur's order to "de-activise" parliament were themselves going against the constitution. The Supreme Court gave no answer to Gus Dur.

The military, however, contended that they had resolved not to be involved in politics. They refused, for example, to be drawn into the conflict between President Abdurrahman Wahid and parliament that resulted in the former's ouster. They neither harkened to his attempt to suspend parliament; nor did they join in the vote against him. They remained righteously neutral.

# CHAPTER 5

# THE ACEH PROBLEM

ANOTHER factor which eventually contributed to the wearing away of Gus Dur's prestige was his languid attitude towards Aceh. Abdurrahman Wahid would have a good understanding of the situation in Aceh, based on its bumpy history. Aceh's location at the strategic northern tip of Sumatra would inevitably make its interests and its reflection of self cast a shadow over the rest of Indonesia.

Even at the beginning of the Christian era a Chinese emperor sent an expedition to the region in which Aceh is located – to obtain a rhinoceros for the imperial zoo. Sumatra has historically been well known for the presence of such animal, including an albino version, although today man's depredations have brought the beast to near extinction. Of all the regions in Indonesia, Aceh was perhaps the first to have contact with the outside world.

Besides the Han zoological venture, Chinese chronicles of the sixth century AD spoke of a northern Sumatran kingdom called Po Li. Ninth-century and later Indian inscriptions and Arabic writings mentioned the area where Aceh is now situated. Venetian traveller Marco Polo, during a voyage past Sumatra, recorded several kingdoms and trading posts on the north of the island. Islam is believed to have reached Aceh very soon after Islam's foundation, but consolidated itself in the following centuries. This showed the energy and maritime reach of the early Moslem proselytisers. Their continued visits for commerce and port calls must have slowly entrenched Islam in the region. Today respectful Muslims refer to Aceh as the verandah to Mecca.

When the Portuguese captured Melaka in 1511, Asian and Arab traders practically shunned the colonial port, and instead brought their business to Aceh. This brought wealth and prosperity to Aceh and ensured its dominance for several decades. During this time Aceh took the lead in constantly attacking Melaka and harrying the Christian Portuguese.

The Acehnese did not confine their belligerence to Christians. They conducted holy wars against their north Sumatran neighbours and took over pepper growing areas, converting the inhabitants to the Muslim faith. Aceh spread its rule or overlordship down Sumatra's west coast, as far as Padang and even across the Melaka Straits to Kedah and other Malay states. Because of Aceh's easy accessibility to the outside world, particularly to the Middle East and Gujerat, Muslim scholars frequently visited it. This strongly confirmed the Acehnese in their Muslim belief and strengthened their religious commitment.

Then came the later rivalries between the European colonial powers, from near the middle of the 17th century, the most sharp being between the Dutch and the British in the 19th. The encroachments of the colonial interests of these two powers grew, especially their rivalry over the tin trade, particularly in Perak.

When Aceh became a Dutch "possession" by agreement with the British at the end of the Napoleonic Wars, a long drawn struggle began in 1873, between the Dutch and Acehnese. The Aceh Wars, lasting intermittently until the Japanese invasion in 1942, were the longest the Dutch ever fought anywhere, and cost them 10,000 lives.

At the beginning of the Dutch attempted takeover in 1873, Dutch military success against Aceh emboldened the Dutch to think that Aceh's ruler would come to terms. But what the sultan might accept was not what his district chiefs and religious leaders (who quarrelled among themselves also) could be constrained to agree to.

Even before the Dutch attack against Aceh actually materialised, rumours appeared to have circulated in Singapore that the Acehnese were seeking connection with other European powers. France, Italy and the United States, and even Japan were mentioned. The Dutch frantically sought assurance from the European powers named that its rights would not be breached, and finally received the required assurances. Whatever lay behind the alleged Acehnese *demarche*, if indeed there had been one, remained a mystery.

It was such proud historical experience that moulded the Acehnese outlook and way of thinking. In modern times, the Free Aceh Movement (Gerakan Aceh Merdeka or GAM) has fought for independence and Islamic rule for Aceh since December 1976. The Indonesian government began military operations, for a time under martial law, against the separatist rebels in 1989. They went on for ten years. The insurgents' zeal for a holy war appeared undampened. Allegations of human rights abuses perpetrated by the Indonesian Armed Forces had also gained more adherents and sympathisers, while the province's indignation over Jakarta's unjust appropriation of Aceh's industrial and economic earnings had reached a peak.

From Jakarta, varied views were expressed about what to do about Aceh. Gus Dur was projecting his cryptic thoughts while travelling. The military wanted to declare martial law in selected areas. Attorney-general Marzuki Darusman proposed multiple layers of dialogue to help restore confidence in the central authority. DPR (House of Representatives) Speaker Akbar Tandjung stressed his opposition to martial law, and insisted on dialogue. General Wiranto, still in office at the germane time, pointed out that there were strong elements in Aceh who did not want to break away from Indonesia. In other words, it was a general babel coming from Jakarta.

On Monday, November 8, 1999, a massive demonstration of Acehnese people demanded a referendum to give them the option to break away from Indonesia. The enormous gathering took place in Acch's capital city, Banda Aceh, in front of the city's principal mosque, Masjid Raya Baiturrahman. Enthusiastic estimates of the multitude that attended the demonstration varied between one and two million. The latter figure would number half of the total population of Aceh.

Later, more sober assessments put the gathering at about half a million, which all the same reflected an impressive display of national feeling. Generally peaceful, all armed personnel having apparently been ordered to stay away, the demonstration – though gigantic – appeared to have proceeded in an atmosphere akin to an extremely hearty Extraordinary General Meeting of a very popular club.

Indeed the meeting was taken as a general sitting of the local Consultative Assembly, chaired by the vice-governor of Aceh, the governor being otherwise engaged in Jakarta, and absent (presumably with apologies). The meeting produced a declaration. It stated that an Open Conference of the Acehnese People's Struggle for self-determination was held on November 8. The rally was organised by the Centre for Aceh Referendum, which included government officers, members of parliament, NGOs, religious leaders, sociopolitical groups, politicians, and so on, and went peacefully.

The report gave the impression that the proceedings appeared to have been undertaken in an ambience of constitutionality. The Declaration was recorded as duly signed by the Provincial Legislative Body, the local governments of all districts in the special territory of Aceh, and by the vice-governor of Aceh. The signatories declared that Acehnese had the right to self-determination through a fair, peaceful and democratic process. A referendum was the only way of achieving such self-determination.

Gus Dur's alternating responses to the challenge posed by the Aceh problem constituted another factor which weakened the president's political image, and added to the irritation he aroused generally. Gus Dur probably had a deeper and more sympathetic understanding of complexities in the Aceh situation than most of his colleagues. The massive demonstration outside the Masjid Raya Baiturrahman was a challenge to Gus Dur's skill in bringing about a solution.

Gus Dur felt that Jakarta should make a move to win the confidence of the Acehnese. He claimed that he would not object to a referendum. He believed that Aceh would opt to remain in Indonesia. For the military, such a stand was too risky to take after what happened to Timor. Other voices were also raised in alarm over Gus Dur's seeming complacence. Wahid himself wanted to gain time so that wiser counsels might prevail.

In the meantime, Teuku Don Zulfahri, secretary-general of the Aceh separatist movement, said that his organisation was ready to negotiate, whenever the Indonesian government agreed. Zulfahri also expressed the view that President Abdurrahman Wahid was consistent and gentlemanly in his attitude towards Aceh, though he also appeared to be delaying the process of settlement. Gus Dur had to keep his cool, because Hasan di Tiro, self-exiled leader of the GAM, had declared that referendum was the only way out.

Zulfahri was speaking from Kuala Lumpur. He said that one condition for talks was that they should be held overseas. Meanwhile, Gus Dur had secured an undertaking from the Aceh rebels for a three-month cessation of hostilities. In early days of his rule, Gus Dur's strategy seemed to be working. GAM's celebration of its 23rd anniversary on December 4, 1999, passed uneventfully, with the independence movement telling residents not to fly the independence flag as originally scheduled.

In mid-February 2000, Gus Dur enunciated a new principle which he called *biar-in-isme*, or laisser-faire-ism, with regard to nerve-wracking happenings in the region. In his controversial way, not giving any indication whether he was speaking tongue-in-cheek, Gus Dur adopted a religio-philosophical stance. He declared that if God wanted the state to crumble, it would. There were problems that had to be solved, and others that would solve themselves. He was getting physically weary with the tasks that confronted him, especially with the murmurings of critics over sectarian and religiously inspired violence.

Returning quickly to a "life is real" attitude, Gus Dur toyed with the idea of a measure of autonomy for Aceh, which had long been in his mind. He was said to be even thinking of integrating GAM into the Indonesian military as a reverse effect of his move at reconciliation. If this was the case, his thoughts were far ahead of the realistic present. The TNI would be laughing grimly, and he would have to come to terms with a credible representation from the Acehnese side. At the same time he would have to convince the Acehnese of his total *bona fides*.

In mid-March, a presidential representative held a meeting with the head of the Free Aceh Movement (GAM). The encounter took place near Pidie, the main stronghold of GAM. But local security forces tried to spoil the attempt at improving the situation by carrying out disturbing searches in the vicinity. Despite such provocations, the government later announced its intention to sign a peace accord with the rebels as a result of which a more humanitarian situation would hopefully emerge in Aceh.

On May 12, 2000, a memorandum of understanding was signed between Indonesian ambassador Hassan Wirayuda and Zaini Abdullah, a GAM representative. This accord was brokered by the Henri Dunant Centre for humanitarian dialogue in Geneva. But by January 2001, when the agreement expired, both sides had been in heavy breach of the accord.

The respective parties had stressed that the agreement was to explore the means to stop the violence in Aceh. GAM, however, stated that while seeking for a peaceful solution, it was determined to push for independence. The Indonesian government made sure that its efforts were not interpreted as a recognition of GAM, nor did it encourage thinking in the direction of independence for Aceh. Instead the government was working towards an equitable settlement under which Aceh would benefit from considerable autonomy, including its decision to impose Islamic law.

In the first three months of 2001, the army reluctantly accepted Abdurrahman Wahid's policy of limited army operations. By May, with Gus Dur coming under severe parliamentary attack and in danger of being replaced as president, the army proceeded with its own preferable option of a military solution. The military went out on an offensive to crush the separatist rebels. It did not remember that, even during the Suharto era, the GAM insurgency flourished because the actions of the military went beyond reasonable limits. Now the very same thing happened. The harsher the military action against Aceh, the more extreme was the insurgent response, until one human rights abuse overtook the other. The bitter conflict extended into Megawati's rule, and brought on her the odium that Gus Dur had suffered.

# CHAPTER 6

# AMBON: ITS HISTORY AND CURRENT DEBACLE

THE conflict in Ambon appears to have started during Habibie's presidency. It was thought that the disturbances in Ambon were deliberately organised to topple Habibie. A quarrel between a taxi-driver and a Muslim Ambonese at the end of Ramadan was used as a pretext for widespread rioting and killing of Christians. It was alleged that security forces simply looked on.

Although several ministers from Habibie's former cabinet were called up for enlightenment on the happenings, the disturbances went on, not only unabated, but with increasing fury. The plight of Ambon appeared to have stemmed from complications of past history and made seemingly intractable by conspiracies of current events. To appreciate the task faced by Gus Dur and Megawati, one needed to understand the full import of the tragic story.

It has been said that the Europeans came to the east to look for Christians and spices. Portuguese, Dutch and English traders quarrelled over rights and opportunities to make huge profits from exporting pepper, clove and nutmeg from the Spice Islands to Europe. What was at that time known as Amboina was the focus of trade rivalry. Maluku was the original Spice Islands. The Dutch valued the Spice Islands so much that they were willing to give up Manhattan to the British, in exchange for possession of a tiny island (Run) in the small Banda Archipelago. It is not known how much they regretted this transaction. Probably as much as the Russians, after they sold Alaska to the Americans for $7 million.

When the Dutch occupied the first of their territorial possessions, which represented the start of their Indies, they had seized them from the Portuguese. But even before the advent of the Portuguese, Maluku had attracted Arab, Indian, Chinese and Japanese traders. These brought their own religious beliefs, but Islam prevailed. With Portuguese influence, Amboina acquired thus a population of Christians as well as Moslems. The Dutch treaty with the local indigenous authority promised freedom of religion. Knowing the brigandage of the times, one may wonder how much of the promise was kept. But Ambonese inherited cultural similarities and ancestral observances were assurances of accord despite religious difference.

The colonial authority favoured the Christians, and the Dutch made fierce and loyal soldiers out of those known as Ambonese. The Ambonese could be regarded as the most pro-Dutch community in the Indies. When the newly created Indonesian Federal Republic was formed in 1949, southern Maluku (capital, Ambon) tried to secede but failed. However, Ambonese exiles continued agitation from Holland. Meanwhile in Maluku itself the Ambonese, who had historically come under the influence of Dutch ways, would be a source of continual concern to Jakarta. The migration from other territories, especially Sulawesi, of other ethnic groups mostly espousing Islam, was organised to water down local Christian dominance.

The Ambonese had been headhunters until early Muslim traders converted them, before the advent of Portuguese and other European colonisers. But any residue of ancestral fierceness would have been subordinated to a sense of group obligation induced by traditional *pela* kinship affiliation. *Pela* (*gandong basudara* = brethren arm-in-arm) was an inter-village bonding system of brotherhood, so close that intermarriage between such sworn kin was regarded as incestuous. *Pela* ensured mutual assistance and mutual hospitality. Despite such close traditional bonding transcending religious affiliation, Christians and Muslims were made to fight and kill one another, and burn each other's homes and churches. It was true that in some areas of Maluku, the inhabitants had only recently emerged from the wild. Des Alwi, a well-known Ambonese himself, and a dominant figure in the Banda islands, recounted how only a few decades back he used to sail close to the shores of Ceram. Then he would encounter primitively clad natives who would suspiciously emerge from the jungle to trade at the water's rim, and quickly disappear on the slightest suspicion of trouble.

But such factors had not previously produced the bloodbath that was soiling, and promising to embroil the whole Indonesian nation and polity. If within the Maluku region, religious differences, a certain backwardness among some tribes, or even the initial migration of new population elements, had not produced social unrest on the current scale, one had to look outside the region for some explanation.

Gus Dur knew as much and had stated so – that gangsters and rowdies recruited by TNI rogue elements, one or two even very highly placed, had gone to Ambon and instigated conflict. Allegedly, the background of these mobsters and their criminal squads was close affiliation to members of the Suharto family. At the same time, circumstances prevailed which were ripe for provocateurs.

The rivalry between the Sultan of Ternate and the Sultan of Tidore, for example, complicated things when the two rulers decided to get themselves involved in "democratic" elections. The Sultan of Ternate had, in history, engaged both Christians and Muslims in his entourage. Because of demographic changes brought about by migration, the ruler found himself having to support the Muslim factions, because they predominated.

TNI rogue elements had more than one item on their agenda of subversion. First of all, they wanted to discredit the new government, and hoped to even sweep into power once more by taking advantage of the weakness of Gus Dur's fledgeling authority. In this they were supported by local and national politicians who, for reasons of their own, wanted a restoration of the previous regime.

A second agenda item would relate to military officers who had been involved in human rights abuses during the *Orde Baru*. They feared that a successful progress to democracy and a clean government would bring them to justice. A third agenda would be that of military officers in sympathy with Islamic fundamentalists and who could manipulate Muslim militants to achieve their ends. Generally, the bulk of the military would not be happy with Gus Dur's efforts to diminish their influence in the affairs of the nation. Islam-oriented officers would resent the trend towards secularism that would be one of the marks of Gus Dur's policy.

Since all dissident groups would have convergent interests, their combined competence in achieving their goals would be high indeed. After unleashing their bandits on to the Maluku scene, which seemed like the preliminary to the main event, the Laskar Jihad were brought in to play. In April 2000, about 3000 Laskar Jihad militia departed for Maluku. No one interdicted their transfer from Jakarta to Ambon. Their leader, Jaffar Umar Thalib, was free to roam anywhere he chose, and utter threats to send more of his holy war fighters. Those on the unfortunate receiving end of *jihad* reported on how relatively well-trained the jihad militia were, and suspected that they also received weapons from the military based locally.

Since the arrival of the Laskar Jihad, more of their troops poured into Maluku. Fighting escalated with military elements just standing by, and not attempting to establish peace. At the same time, even police posts were attacked without the army coming to their aid. The Laskar Jihad has spread its terror to other parts of east Indonesia, right up to Irian Jaya.

Long before the situation in Maluku became generally uncontrollable, meetings and large demonstrations were held in Jakarta to protest against Gus Dur's inability to deal with the mayhem in Ambon. Very probably those protesting vigorously included the very groups who were responsible for the conflict in Maluku. Fuad Bawazier, one of those agitating for Gus Dur's removal, attended a mass rally of 100,000 militants at Monas (the National Monument) in January 2000. He was also accused of funding the Laskar Jihad in Maluku. The whole purpose of these actions was to enfeeble the position of the president and vice-president.

# CHAPTER 7

# THE GROWING INFLUENCE OF ISLAM

THE turmoil in Maluku was not only to bring about instability directed at revealing President Abdurrahman Wahid's incompetence. Sectarian violence was not an unfamiliar phenomenon, even in Suharto's time. Reportedly, nearly 600 churches were destroyed during Suharto's and Habibie's time. The assault on, and razing of, churches had therefore been a growing phenomenon. There were also a number of mosques which were torched by Christians.

This simmering Christian-Muslim antagonism seemed even to have affected Suharto, particularly when the Christian Benny Murdani had the temerity to advise the president that the first family's children were engaged in excessive corruption. President Suharto slowly began to show greater favour to so-called "green" generals, of Islamic persuasion. The pogrom in Maluku and elsewhere was directed towards redressing the population balance in favour of Muslims"– where previously Christians had been in the majority.

It was therefore suspected that the creation of a creeping coup was not only to enable the secret generals to come to power, as a result of widespread instability possibly leading to chaos, but also sooner or later, to harken to the calls for an Islamic state. There would not be any basic conflict with the notion of a unitary state. All that was needed was for Pancasila (the basic Indonesian philosophy of the unitary state) to be modified. Such an analysis explains the activities of the "*tangan jahat*" (literally, bad hands; unruly elements controlled by some figures in the TNI) that caused such ructions within the Indonesian polity.

The ground among the *rakyat* appeared more and more prepared for such Islamisation. Poverty had increased. Basri Hasanudin, minister for eradication of poverty, knew this. The figure for the poor in Indonesia had risen to nearly 80 million by end-1999. The per capita income of US$1,000 was reduced to far less than half. Unemployment had soared because of the closure of manufacturing plants. Many parents could not send their children to school. Unrest in the provinces had also affected people's welfare.

Rural misery drove people to the cities, swelling urban dissatisfaction and restlessness. Unemployed youths and men flocked to mosques because they had nothing better to do. The Muslim religious centres provided social and spiritual solace. In such a way was Islamisation of the *abangan* taking place. The *abangan* were original Muslims inclined to animism and profoundly affected by Javanese culture and belief. Many of them would have belonged to the Nadlatul Ulama.

Thus, religion was assuming different significance in the minds of those who had chosen to dwell in the cities. But inevitably a slum existence would, in cases, also tend to radicalise such a mindset. In the centre, the cry of affiliation with the perceived plight of Muslims in the regions grew more determined to resolve into action like *jihad* and *jihad* warriors – *laskar jihad*. It was sad that the political designs of those fuelling the conflict in Maluku involved feeding the fires of religious hatred. Sadder still was the intention of asserting the supremacy of Islam through might of arms.

# CHAPTER 8

# GUS DUR FLIRTS WITH FEDERALISM

GUS DUR'S influence over the large and moderate Nadlatul Ulama required him to be fingered as an enemy. His impotence over the happenings in east Indonesia, coupled with what seemed to be his waffling over Aceh, prepared further the ground for his eventual removal.

Amien Rais, general-secretary of the National Mandate Party (PAN), was the one during Gus Dur's regime who had been insistent in raising the question of federalism. He thought that it was the best state form for Indonesia at the current time. Amien declared so, despite the fact that most of his PAN supporters would not be behind him on that issue. Some thought that it was out of political vanity that Amien expressed such a view. Was he deliberately pursuing an eccentric line?

Particularly strong and negative was the reaction from vice-president Megawati Sukarnoputri's Indonesian Democratic Struggle Party (PDI-P). Megawati very clearly declared her rejection of the federal form of government. She firmly avowed that the unitary state of Indonesia was the final condition. A similar reaction came from several other segments of society. But the debate went on.

One such reaction came from former Home Affairs Minister, Rudini. He said that the federal concept would simply worsen the national condition, if presently implemented. He spoke at a seminar that referred to the dilemma of demands for referendum and the aspiration for freedom. Rudini said dismissively that the current time was not appropriate for such a discussion. What was needed was work and development. The condition of the Indonesian nation was not normal. The economy had to be built first. Moreover, such discussion needed prolonged debate, and demanded time to resolve.

In Singapore, press commentaries on the subject of an Indonesian federal system reflected the mood projected by Rudini. The newspaper observations were correct about a split on this issue. But to majority, powerful conservative forces, which included the armed forces and more or less a mass of adherents to Muslim organisations, federalism was a no-no. If the independence-aspiring provinces insisted on referendums to determine their political destiny, the consequence would be the military stepping in with hard outcomes. Such was Gus Dur's dilemma.

If one could read through the president's contradictory affirmations on the subject, a federal system which Germany or the United States had, was out of the question. It would simply spell the doom of Indonesia as a national entity. But Gus Dur appeared to think of a subtle way out of his dilemma. "Federalism" would be a devolution not taking the form of a united states of Indonesia. The form chosen would be autonomy with different ingredients for different regions. One of the ingredients would, of course, be greater participation in the disposal of income from regional resources. But Gus Dur was not convinced that the population in the provinces was sufficiently united and technically competent to finally insist on complete devolution. For example, even in Aceh, the Free Aceh Movement (GAM) was not characterised by a singleness of purpose. Hasan di Tiro was old and feeble. The commanders under him were in conflict with one another. It was history – which the Dutch encountered – repeating itself. A corresponding situation prevailed in other provinces harking after independence.

The real problem was that agitators and provocateurs were at work stirring strife. For example, what was Yorrys Raweyai, allegedly a well-known provocationist, doing in West Irian, helping to raise the secessionist, independence flag there? Was Yorrys an ardent secessionist? Yorrys' allegiance was also well-known – it was for the Suharto establishment. It was believed that provocation was occurring in Aceh too. The term *orang tidak kenal* (OTK), meaning unknown persons, was having a respectable place in the local vocabulary of conflict.

The president could not but see his task of settling the Aceh crisis through negotiation as crucial for his own reputation. Aceh would stand as a test for other regions, which were toying with the idea of separation. Settle the Aceh problem by whatever means, but leave it still remaining as part of the Indonesian nation, and the other segments starting on their centrifugal whirl would slow down their action and follow Aceh's example.

# The Saga Of Tommy Suharto

The situation in Indonesia towards the end of the year 2000 showed how dominant confusion was. In September 2000, the Indonesian Supreme Court found Hutomo Mandala Putra, aka Tommy Suharto, guilty of corruption and of defrauding the state of over US$10 million. Tommy asked for a presidential pardon. A stay of execution was granted. The convicted man was reported to have met President Gus Dur at the Borobodur Hotel privately on October 7 and 8. Before the meeting, Gus Dur declared that he would reject any clemency plea. But except for accusations that Gus Dur had made a deal with Tommy, nothing seemed to have come out of the Borobodur meeting. Attempts to arrest Tommy met with all sorts of prevarication from all quarters.

The super-power shadows behind Tommy were intimidating. Eventually he went into hiding. There must have been powerful figures sheltering him. Unsubstantiated rumours mentioned Wiranto; other gossip referred to retired general Hartono, close friend of the Suharto family, as shielding the fugitive. Tommy remained in hiding for about a year, during which time the original Supreme Court decision which had convicted Tommy, was overturned. The corruption case against Tommy was dismissed, but other charges of alleged murder of the judge who convicted him, and of illegal arms possession were raised.

The saga of Tommy Suharto was one prolonged episode showing how Gus Dur's foes could fairly easily mock at, and taunt, the president, and spoil his image in the eyes of the people, and thus contribute to his downfall. Tommy could escape the clutches of the law, during Gus Dur's time. But Megawati's rule saw, quite early, how the miscreant was captured and made to face his sentence for conspiracy to commit murder.

The search for Tommy took time. Even the houses of some generals were thoroughly rummaged. Were the police a little scared of going too far in their efforts to locate Tommy? They remembered that Wiranto was minister for defence and security when Suharto was still in power. Wiranto had undertaken to attend to the safety and security of the president's family, should anything happen to Suharto. Moreover there was Prabowo, Tommy's brother-in-law, and also Djaja Suparman who was close to Wiranto. Such was the formidable cohort that could be expected to be Tommy's guardians.

# CHAPTER 9

# THE CHRISTMAS EVE
# BOMBINGS

AT the end of the year 2000, a Christmas celebration by the *tangan jahat* (unruly elements of the TNI) took the form of a series of bomb attacks against churches. These were obviously designed to show the power of the *tangan jahat*. The details of the bombings were given wide media coverage and some interesting characteristics emerged.

Care was taken to keep damage and casualties to a minimum. Bombs were exploded outside houses of worship. Inside, except for brief terror, services went on as usual. Outside, people were injured and killed: food-vendor, chauffeur, lounger, police officers who tried to tamper with explosive material. Vehicles were destroyed or badly damaged.

There was an uneven spread of casualties. In Medan city, nearly a dozen bombs were found or reported. Most were disguised as gift packages, and addressed to individuals. None of the bombs exploded and caused damage to people or property. Some bombs – arranged them like targets in a shooting gallery – were exploded by the police.

Of all the locations where the bombs were laid, Riau suffered the worst. Pekan Baru and Batam suffered more than half of the 90 or so injured, and nearly one-third of the total killed. Medan fronts Malaysia; Riau, especially Batam, fronts Singapore.

Gus Dur condemned the bombings, and said they were meant to cripple his already ailing government. Other deadly bombings had taken place earlier in the year. In August, two people were killed when a bomb exploded outside the Philippines ambassador's residence. In September, a car bomb blew up in the basement parking lot of Jakarta's Stock Exchange. Fifteen people were killed in the explosion and the fire that followed. The bombings were like a bombardment against the background of the bloody war in Maluku.

Who could have inspired the terrorist actions? Could a group of former generals and pro-Suharto elite, whose unifying characteristics were their radical (or extremist) Islamic espousal, hatred for Christians and hatred for Chinese shed light on the subject? One of the most notable among these was Ahmad Sumargono, a leader in the Islamic Crescent and Star political party (PBB), the hard-line Indonesian Committee for World Islamic Solidarity (KISDI), and was associated with the Front Pembela Islam (FPI).

Sumargono is unashamedly and rabidly pro-Islamic in his pronouncements. He declared once that he would support any group or measure that was pro-Islam, regardless of whether it was right or wrong. One could better see in Sumargono aspects of the *wayang kulit* figure Kumbakarna, who would fight for his country under any circumstances. The question is, was Sumargono more *wayang* than reality?

Sumargono's carefully-trimmed beard, well-dressed and dapper appearance, and display of a high sense of humour, are ironic contrasts to his own description of his followers as demoniacs. He has had attached to himself descriptions like "*the most dangerous man, extrim, garang, radikal*". Sumargono's three-storied home has been the venue of meetings before demonstrations. Prabowo Subianto and Fadli Zon, both despisers of Christians and Chinese, have been his guests. But the actual involvement of such figures had to be ruled out, because of the later discovery that the perpetrators of the Bali bombings in 2002 were also guilty of the Christmas Eve 2000 attacks.

Just for the record, Fadli Zon was apparently a close associate of Prabowo, for he invariably acted as his spokesman before the media. Fadli Zon spoke loudly about Prabowo's lack of interest in politics. But Fadli Zon was his sidekick, who tried secretly to position Prabowo to take over the radical Crescent and Moon Party (PBB) from Yusril Ihza Mahendra. PBB would thus become Prabowo's political base.

Many asked what Prabowo was doing in Jakarta around January 15, 2001. This was the day on which large-scale riots were anticipated, but appeared to be squashed by a ponderous military response. It was fancied that, had the rioting occurred, Prabowo would have suddenly appeared, rising above the internecine contest between rival Muslims, as a sort of super-Muslim.

It was odd that immediately after the Christmas bombings, it was at Prabowo Subianto that accusing fingers were pointed. In January 2001, Prabowo denied at a press conference that he had had anything to do with the Christmas bombings. He accused certain circles of character-assassination. He said that he had informed the president Gus Dur so, that there were people who wanted to spoil his (Prabowo's) good name. Prabowo thanked some police officials who had stated firmly that there were no indications that he had been involved in the Christmas bombings. Another name receiving media attention over alleged links with the Christmas bombings was former army chief Hartono. He angrily repudiated the smear.

Whether they were related or not, in May-June of 2000, a series of "secret" meetings were held in hotels and other (residential) locations between

Wiranto and his followers (*kelompok-nya*). Of course the "report" of such clandestine plottings came to light mysteriously.

The meetings allegedly discussed highly absorbing matters: to order line-ups in the military; to deflate Gus Dur's rule and seize the government; play up Buloggate and Bruneigate, which was hotting up the political climate; penetration of the press to weaken Gus Dur and supporters; readying terror, including bombing tactics, in various cities; instigate the Front for the Defence of Islam (FPI) and Laskar Jihad to take secret steps to weaken Gus Dur's supporters; pressure the supporters of Amien Rais (central Islamic groupings) and Akbar Tandjung (Golkar) to support Wiranto; pressure Panglima Widodo into believing that Wiranto was still strong in the TNI; and similar conversational items.

These meetings could be no more than discussions to unseat Gus Dur. On the other hand, they could have been more than simply political. The participants at the meetings were duplicates of Sumargono. Fuad Bawazier was a close crony of Suharto, having been finance minister in Suharto's time. During the Muslim-Christian troubles in Maluku, Fuad Bawazier was said to have financed the despatch of Jihad warriors to stir up more violence in the troubled areas. Bawazier was himself a radical Muslim with great experience as a political engineer. His financing of the Jihad to Maluku, it was claimed, was to bring Gus Dur down. He would continue to feature right into Megawati's time.

Gus Dur's rule had from the beginning evoked querulousness and opposition. Voices raised against Gus Dur became more and more strident. Golkar, as a leading political party and with its history going deep into Suharto time and territory, was loud in its criticism of Gus Dur's alleged involvement in two financial scandals.

Gus Dur could also play dirty. His political stronghold was East Java. In early February 2001 Abdurrahman Wahid's supporters, enraged by Golkar's ridicule of Gus Dur's erratic rule, in their thousands attacked Golkar's offices in two towns in the heartland of East Java. The president went to East Java to calm his supporters.

But in March and May 2001, some hundreds of students sealed up two of Fuad Bawazier's houses, accusing him of corruption. Bawazier feared such further agitation against him. It seems that it was Gus Dur who had inspired these threatening moves. After Gus Dur was displaced by Megawati, police arrested a man in Jakarta. He had been caught red-handed with several home-made bombs at the Hotel Mega on Jalan Proklamasi, according to a mid-November report.

The arrested man, Kesman, alleged that he had obtained the explosives during Abdurrahman Wahid's time in order to protect Bawazier. It was not clear how Kesman intended to use bombs to protect Bawazier who, he told police, had recruited him. After Gus Dur's political demise on 23 July 2001, apparently such action as Kesman planned was not required any more.

So the small-time bomber sought to hide his cache of explosives. He originally thought of secreting the bombs in Bawazier's house in west Jakarta. But he feared police road-block searches for drugs would reveal his illegal possession. So he decided on hiding his explosive contraband in the Hotel Mega, where he was caught.

# CHAPTER 10

# THE ECLIPSE OF GUS DUR'S LEADERSHIP

IT WAS not found necessary to use bombs to unseat Abdurrahman Wahid. In the end, he unseated himself. When he entered the presidential palace, people were full of hope for his rule. It was thought that he was the one man who could engineer a coalition of political support. But very early in his presidential career, both supporters and opponents began to view Gus Dur's progress with dismay. It started with his constant travels. During one of such trips, he played out his dismissal of General Wiranto with uncertain drama. From this time on, he incurred the suspicion and resentment of the military. Democratic transformation, on which so many had pinned their hopes, was stymied by Gus Dur's own eccentric, unpredictable and autocratic behaviour. He had brought to his rule too much of the style of patriarchal governance which he used over the Nadlatul Ulama, whose 30 million Muslim adherents regarded him as father.

In his lofty self-regard that he should be above suspicion, he got involved in a personal scandal. His chauffeur absconded with state funds. The odium fell on his employer, Abdurrahman Wahid. Gus Dur himself could be accused of at least not exercising due vigilance in the disposal of funds donated by the Sultan of Brunei. Wahid was accused of misappropriation. The evidence of such wrongdoing was circumstantial against Gus Dur. But Parliament was ready to censure him, despite his own personal pleas of his hands being clean. Both parliament and Gus Dur drew their lines of attack and defence. Even with about only six weeks before likely impeachment hearings, the lines could not be said to be final. Gus Dur still had stamina. And he may have had the impression that he could put his opponents on the defensive.

Theirs had been a policy and campaign of continuous complaint, criticism, denigration, and of pre-judgement and threat. This started with queries about Gus Dur's frequent travels and absences from his post. It went on through the dismissal of Wiranto to the seemingly endless sequence of cabinet and ministerial changes that Gus Dur wrought.

Gus Dur's double-talk, as well as his blunt and aggressive frankness dismayed and angered his antagonists. They became united against him, even swinging Megawati to their side, allowing her to emerge as their champion and their choice to succeed Abdurrahman Wahid.

The president's debonair, *kampong* attitude towards money brought two charges – Buloggate and Bruneigate – against him. Although Gus Dur's involvement was actually only surmised, the House of Representatives (DPR) took it as proven. In Bruneigate, Gus Dur was accused of receiving a gift of US$2 million from the Sultan of Brunei. Abdurraman Wahid stated that the money had been obtained to assist humanitarian agencies doing work in Aceh. But the nub of criticism was over the fact that Gus Dur should not have acted in a personal capacity. Buloggate was the accusation that Gus Dur assisted in the misdirection of US$4 million from the funds of Bulog, a state agency for the logistics control of foodstuffs.

The DPR went through proceedings for calling a special session of the MPR. Realising that grounds for impeachment were feeble, if it stuck to accusations about misconduct in money matters, the DPR added a further allegation of incompetence in office. Apparently, the legislators wanted to get Gus Dur by all means.

Gus Dur tried to negotiate with the legislators. He sent a team of three highest-ranking officials: defence minister Mahfud, Attorney-General Baharudin Lopa and coordinating minister Agum Gumelar, to meet the parliamentarians. One of the conditions Gus Dur set was that the MPR special session should not discuss the competence of his administration.

Gus Dur's condition was turned down. Discussion of financial misconduct could be objectively determined by a respectable judicial judgement. And such judgement had already been delivered by the Supreme Court in Gus Dur's favour. It would be easy to guess that evaluation of competence would be highly subjective. All the more would it be attractive to Gus Dur's foes. The conciliation team continued their ferrying up and down on their negotiations.

Vainly the president confronted his principal opponents with the possibility of being charged with corruption. But some elements among the parlimentarians were trying to hasten the meeting of the MPR to an earlier date. This could result in street protests. Already workers in several cities had begun to demonstrate against labour service conditions which, they challenged, discriminated against them and indeed favoured employers. Apparently the workers found the president sympathetic to their cause. For their demonstrations in Jakarta appeared directed towards Megawati.

In Bandung, West Java, demonstrators in their thousands rioted. The media reported that rioters invaded the provincial legislative building, and broke windows, and set fire to furniture and documents. Vehicles too were set alight. In an industrial town near Surabaya, workers stoned factories and caused serious traffic blockages. The provincial legislature was also stormed, after the workers succeeded in entering Surabaya. Still the workers knew it was all, as one remarked, a game between parliament and Gus Dur.

Another source of unhappiness to the *rakyat* was the issue of fuel price hikes. The government had announced it would delay the implementation of price increases for fuel – for an uncertain period. It was mindful that sharp price rises had triggered riots and violent demonstrations, which toppled Suharto three years back. This time round the government had tried to present itself as the *rakyat's* friend and champion.

But Gus Dur's government had to face reality. The government *had* to implement the fuel hikes – on Saturday June 16. Massive demonstrations followed. The parliamentarians automatically blamed Gus Dur. They used this as an excuse for wanting to expedite the calling of MPR's special session. Gus Dur responded by declaring that any earlier dating of the special session would prompt him to declare a condition of emergency. The scenario of developing social and political unrest could give Gus Dur grounds to persuade a reluctant military to shed their coyness and move in to restore order.

The military were not ready to be put to the test. They were still badly divided. They shrunk from a tandem with Gus Dur. They would have preferred Megawati as partner. Army chief Endriartono Sutarto instructed that only orders from the president that were constitutionally lawful need be obeyed.

Still it was not yet clear whether Gus Dur might yet manoeuvre the military to his side. For one, he tried to severely limit the options for the other side. One of the principal means, he thought, was to declare that not under any circumstances would he resign. He told the media that, if parliament proceeded to impeach him, the people would rise up. If he decided to hunker down in the presidential place, troops would be in a quandary. Gus Dur may have imagined thousands of disgruntled rakyat demonstrating, swelled by masses of workers. Dissatisfaction in the provinces would complicate the situation. But it did not turn out that way.

The reality was that the lawmakers were going ahead with plans to bring forward the People's Assembly meeting. They also had their vision – that Gus Dur would hasten away, and Megawati would take over, and inaugurate an era of democracy and justice.

But it seemed at that time that each side was racing to try and launch a pre-emptive strike ahead of the other, and prevent an injurious setback. The parliamentarians wanted to deny Gus Dur time to sow confusion and discord within their ranks, which was not so solid as superficial indications might convey. The strongest parties, Golkar and PDI-P, had fissures within their ranks. But sadly for Gus Dur, these would only appear later after Megawati had taken over.

Some feared that Gus Dur was already positioned to take advantage among the masses. Wahid might even succeed in forcing the military to accede to a declaration of emergency, on grounds of serious social disturbance. On another front, Gus Dur seemed about to consolidate his position by directing the Attorney-General towards investigating Akbar Tandjung and other figures from the new order regime. Even action against Tandjung would have some effect in Megawati's future time.

Gus Dur also withdrew the suspension of prosecution against Marimutu Sinivasan of Texmaco notoriety. Sinivasan had allegedly obtained favourable bank loans through his friendship with Suharto. Abroad, reportedly for medical treatment, were Prajogo Pangestu and Sjamsul Nursalim, both wanted for investigation into graft allegations. Lower House member Nurdin Khalid, from Golkar, was already being interrogated for corruption.

Bombs also exploded in an empty room of a two-storey boarding house in South Jakarta. The mystery of these explosions, whose material consisted of high explosives but without a detonation agency, baffled police and added to public anxiety and confusion.

Within his twenty-one months of holding power, Wahid had to face a formidable host of antagonists and hostile actions. He had been ready to bring about democracy, institute justice and openness and stamp out corruption. Gus Dur showed tolerance at the beginning of his regime. But the powers arraigned against him were too strong. They could be summed up as the haunting by Suharto and the left-over poison of his new order generals and politicians which was too difficult to suck out of the system.

But Gus Dur's own character, described as enigmatic, whimsical and mercurial, contributed to his own downfall. At first his erratic behaviour and his fund of jokes put his enemies off-guard. His unpredictability was shown especially by his off-on decision to dismiss General Wiranto. But his success in doing so antagonised a whole slew of past and present TNI power holders. Alert, they subverted his moves towards military reform which would have hurt the interests of many generals.

In the end even his supporters looked on him as a bizarre liability, as judged by Susilo Bambang Yudhoyono leaving Wahid's side, almost at the last minute, and joining Megawati. The House of Representatives had asked Gus Dur to share power with Megawati, his vice-president, as a condition for him to continue as president until 2004. Gus Dur responded by declaring that Megawati did not have the ability to rule. Indeed there was not even a suitable candidate to be president. Before this Wahid had sacked (besides Wiranto and earlier Hamzah Haz) two economic ministers, and arrested the governor of the Central Bank on suspicion of corruption. Such had been his peremptory style.

Under such circumstances, Yudhoyono finally felt that he did not have any option but to throw his weight also behind Megawati. The House of

Representatives had issued an ultimatum to Gus Dur at the end of April. He had within a month to give an explanation of the Bruneigate and Buloggate allegations as well as give an undertaking to improve his performance. Yudhoyono was assessing Abdurrahman Wahid correctly when he sadly concluded that Gus Dur would play a mad game stubbornly right to the end. The TNI was alarmed by Gus Dur's anticipated antics. The military was divided, and did not have any outstanding or charismatic figure who could lead the country. It feared civil disruption that an increasingly arrogant president might cause. What the TNI decided on was to applaud a transition from Gus Dur to Megawati, and hence to confidentially support the step by step moves of parliament to reject Gus Dur and appoint Megawati Sukarnoputri.

By the end of May, there was still defiance from Gus Dur. After this, he threatened again and again to declare a state of emergency, in order to dissolve the MPR. On July 23, 2001, the Indonesian People's Consultative Assembly in turn impeached and sacked Abdurrahman Wahid, and chose Megawati Sukarnoputri to be the new leader. Gus Dur now refused to accept the MPR's impeachment decision, and withdrew into the presidential palace behind a barbed wire barricade.

If Gus Dur expected tens of thousands of Nadlatul Ulama adherents to come out in his support, as he holed up behind razor-wire barricades in the palace, he was mistaken. Gus Dur found that he had very little support even from his own Nadlatul Ulama as well as the National Awakening Party, which he had founded. The thousands had been given other instructions to hold still. Both organisations had apparently cautioned their supporters to take it easy. Only a few hundred die-hards kept vigil outside the presidential palace. No troops were out in force to face thousands. Discreet patrols of panzers found the populace quiet.

Ironically, during Gus Dur's self-imposed siege, he received a visit from Megawati's new vice-president, Hamzah Haz. Gus Dur soon accepted the inevitable. On July 25, 2001, former president Abdurrahman Wahid quit the palace for a favourite activity – a trip abroad. Apparently with his country's blessings, he went to Baltimore, Maryland in the US for medical treatment. *Sic transit gloria mundi.*

# CHAPTER 11

# MEGAWATI BEGINS HER RULE

WHEN Megawati Sukarnoputri took over the reins of government from Abdurrahman Wahid, political confusion was at its most rife. Indonesia was the world's fourth most populous nation, 210 million strong, and the largest Muslim nation in the world. Economically, Indonesia had not yet recovered from the 1997 world recession, whose effects had been made worse by events in 1998 surrounding the calamitous downfall of the Suharto regime. Gus Dur's unpredictable style, and chiefly the antagonism he had aroused among the military, did nothing to ease the Indonesian predicament. Megawati admitted: "We face disintegration, whether it's territorial, social or economical. We face a future where reform is being halted." (Source: CNN, August 10, 2001)

Megawati was as popular with the Indonesian people, at the time of her accession, as much as Gus Dur was not. In fact, the situation could be envisioned as a zero sum game. What Gus Dur had lost, Megawati had won. What really Gus Dur had failed in, was to retain the support of the military establishment *and* the ruling elite with their control of powerful alliances. This support had swung on to Megawati's side.

In appearance, parliament had dismissed Gus Dur. In a repeat of history, parliament was able to do this because the military, behind the scenes, had allowed it. Just as the military was instrumental in having Habibie removed. This was the third time a new president came in by default. It was interesting that the political elite (including part of the Muslim establishment which could not brook a woman becoming president) that had prevented Megawati from becoming president at the end of 1999, was the same who obtained her victory this time.

Megawati's accession was welcomed internationally. Singapore, especially, felt glad. Megawati's two predecessors had, towards the end of their truncated regimes, taken an acrimonious attitude towards Singapore. Hope was expressed all round that democratic reforms would ensue and action would be taken against corruption.

While interested observers watched, the fifth president moved to form her cabinet, which she described as *gotong-royong*, or mutual cooperation. In terms of aura, the *rakyat* looked on Megawati as the daughter of Sukarno, the father of the Indonesian nation. Her team of technocrats and experienced politicians was given enthusiastic reception. Her vice-president Hamzah Haz smiled as she called for unity. The biggest challenges were corruption and the economy. Megawati would announce her choice of Attorney-General soon. Ties with the IMF had to be warmed up. They had been frozen.

Megawati, a short while later, named State Enterprises Minister Laksamana Sukardi as head of the bank re-structuring agency (IBRA), which had been previously supervised by the finance minister. However finance minister Boediono would concentrate on the budget. After the turmoil during Abdurrahman Wahid's last few weeks in office, many expressed hope that reform could be headed by Sukardi with his charge of US$66 billion worth of assets in IBRA.

The president expressed regret to resource-rich Aceh and Irian Jaya at the western and eastern ends of the country, for the conflicts that had lent themselves to human rights abuses. But she warned that secession was out of the question. This had always been her standard position. But this view had not received universal, especially regional, support.

In early 2001, Gus Dur had cobbled together some legislation on regional autonomy and revenue sharing. A 1974 law had ensured that the central government controlled everything: appointments of governors, mayors and even heads of districts. Agriculture, religion, education and so on had been controlled from the centre. Although the provinces still bitterly criticised the new legislation, it was a significant advance on the old.

The revenue sharing law was intended to redress the balance between what the provinces gave to the centre and what they were allowed to derive as revenue from their own resources. Yet provincial authorities complained that the new law had loopholes which the central government could exploit.

A suggestion for a federal constitutional arrangement, such as had always been supported by Amien Rais, raised cries of agreement in some of the resource-rich provinces. But political parties, legislators and the military plus Megawati herself battened down on this move. And less reputable elements seemed ready to take the law into their own hands. The assassination of Theys Eluay may have had some connection with the Papuan leader's cry of a free Papua.

What was wrong with the agitated situation in the provinces was that it was not spontaneous. It had been complicated by the involvement of forces and elements outside the provinces, and even outside Indonesia itself. For example, the *Jakarta Post* reported on September 30, 2001 that fundamentalist groups in Malaysia had sent fighters to Ambon. Also, one recollects that a Malaysian was seriously wounded in a premature bomb explosion in Jakarta. Ethno-religious conflicts had become a trans-national problem. Sectarian sentiment translating itself into militant action was crossing national, in addition to crossing, provincial boundaries.

For example, the Laskar Jihad had transported thousands of its "soldiers", its well-trained militia, from Java to Ambon. There it played a very partisan role, by siding with Muslim communities against the Christians. Who were the controllers of the Laskar Jihad and similar private armies? Allegedly a covey of top pro-Suharto generals including Wiranto even, and close colleagues like Djadja Suparman may be the ultimate answer.

Other names to qualify as *dalangs* pulling strings could be Kivlan Zein (background), Agum Gumelar (serving in Megawati's August 9 cabinet), even Hendropriyono (retired but returned to active role as chief of intelligence). Hendropriyono was a mystifying figure. He had taken, and apparently still took, a qualified stance against restless Muslim fundamentalist elements. It was apparently those in such a category who opposed the government and its policies that earned Hendropriyono's wrath.

Simply, the TNI could be separated into those who sought to be professionals, like Endriartono Sutarto and Agus Widjojo, and those who played politics. Perhaps in the latter class could be placed those like Hendropriyono, Wiranto, Tyasno Sidarto, and Hartono. Hartono could be particularly singled out for his closeness to the Suharto clan because of his friendship with Suharto's daughter Tutut.

If a general played politics, he would be isolated if he played the game by himself. He would inevitably belong to a power-playing group. These powerful figures maintained a respectful relationship with fallen dictator, Suharto. The Suharto clan had all the time integrated their interests with powerful military elements and influential civil servants and politicians. Throughout the regime of Abdurrahman Wahid and now with Megawati, the *status quo* prevailed.

The power and influence of the political generals rested also on their wealth. This they derived from the corporations that they managed, formally on behalf of the TNI. Such businesses were necessary for the TNI to operate as a reasonably efficient organisation. What the government doled out was woefully inadequate. It was not so much the principle of the military being involved in business, as the transparency in which such operations were transacted and the audit and controls exercised, that needed to be questioned. During her first year in office, President Megawati's attempts to cut out the corruption of wealth and power did not produce laudable results. Reforms aimed at democratisation also jerked to a stop. Gus Dur had tried to bring the military under civilian control. Megawati returned power to the military elements. But early auguries were not good. A Supreme Court judge was murdered; a bombing took place at a Senen plaza; and police seized a cache of guns, ammunition and grenades at the rented houses inhabited by Tommy Suharto, who had disappeared.

# The Saga Of Tommy Suharto Continues

Could it be that the capture of Tommy Suharto at this stage, when he could not be apprehended during Gus Dur's time, was *wayang* designed to enhance Megawati's good image. In September 2000, the Indonesian Supreme Court had found Hutomo Mandala Putra, aka Tommy Suharto, guilty of corruption and of defrauding the state of over US$10 million. Tommy had asked for a presidential pardon. Tommy's lawyers were intrepid people. The convicted man was said to have had a confidential meeting with Gus Dur at the Borobudur Hotel on October 7 and 8. Apparently the condition of the Indonesian legal system allowed this.

Gus Dur had declared that he would reject any clemency plea, but nothing seemed to have come out of the Borobudur Hotel meeting, except accusations that Gus Dur had made a deal with Tommy. Attempts to arrest Tommy met with prevarication from all sorts of quarters.

A year after Tommy went into hiding, the police were still hunting down the deft escapee. During this time, the original Supreme Court decision convicting Tommy was overturned. The corruption case was dismissed. But other charges of alleged murder of the judge who had convicted Tommy were raised, as well as illegal possession of arms.

They finally arrested him in a large, rented house in a residential suburb in South Jakarta, on November 28, 2001. They had been tracking him for over a week, using special electronic equipment to trace calls from his mobile phone. Tommy had been in constant telephone contact with a reportedly pregnant girlfriend.

But there were other women, it was said, who visited Tommy in his house of refuge. According to personal accounts, the police had been watching the house, which Tommy had rented. They had made discreet enquiries with neighbours and ultimately with the house-owner, saying that they were looking for drug-dealers. When they finally raided the premises, they had to go through several rooms of the capacious dwelling before they came across Tommy sleeping.

Without his moustache Tommy was still smiling. But he seemed less jubilant than in photos taken during his playboy heyday, although he did not appear too worried. He was reported as having been embraced by the police chief, though some averred that this was not true. What was true they said was that the national police chief, Bimantoro, embraced the Jakarta police boss in exhilaration, for the good work that had been achieved, practically on the last day of Bimantoro's active service. But fingers were also quick to point at Tommy not being cuffed, and apparently being given special treatment, such as being allowed to participate in a press conference after his arrest.

Indonesia's Foreign Minister, Hassan Wirajuda, claimed that Tommy's

arrest showed the Indonesian government's serious intention of upholding
the law. Others sneered at the capture and thought the show to be a "police
party", and that the *wayang* was an elaborate performance to let Tommy off.
However the powers that be decided that the *wayang* had gone far enough.
Megawati had to be shown as upholding the law.

The prosecutors demanded a fifteen-year sentence! For masterminding
the murder of a Supreme Court judge? Tommy was thus sentenced, and was
at first sent to a prison where he enjoyed amenities like air-conditioning comfort
and a room with a view. He was later transferred to a maximum security prison,
where he had a room next to Bob Hasan, a good friend of the old Suharto.
Hasan had been sentenced to six years' imprisonment for corruption. Both
Tommy and Bob said they were interested in studying Islam.

In the early course of the incarceration of both Tommy and Hasan,
they were given a very brief (a few months) reduction of their sentence, resulting
from Indonesia's national celebrations

# CHAPTER 12

---

# WHEN WILL INDONESIA CHANGE?

WAS Indonesia mired too deep in its governmental and political morass (and manipulation by powerful and ruthless generals with their own agenda) to be able to correct itself, so as to contribute to the security and political stability of the region? Disasters hit a passive polity. Floods in February 2002 inundated the capital city and caused widespread social and financial grief. Over 300,000 persons had been displaced in the floods, nearly 150 died, and hundreds of homes had been destroyed.

Jakarta Governor Sutiyoso merely declared the floods a natural disaster. But it was really the result of years of neglecting the drainage system and a lack of evironmental control. Blocked drains had been ignored and development projects had burgeoned unrestrictedly, to the profit of land exploiters.

The people had lost faith in their leaders. Already they were resorting to vigilante tactics against common law-breakers. Robbers, for example, were beaten up by indignant villagers or town-dwellers, sometimes to death. People were rapidly losing hope in the government's ability to deal out justice and right wrongs.

A recent media survey revealed how fed up people were of political reports. They craved for entertainment instead. As a result, for example, talk shows on political issues lost their prime time slots. As a further example, it was commented that consumers wanted to know how East Timorese felt about their independence, not what government officials were saying about the "facts". Consumers who had been rendered passive by years of propaganda were more keen on the human interest side of events.

Perhaps the primary cause of Indonesia's slide was corruption – which had become pervasive from Suharto's time to the present day. The Tommy Suharto episode was one eminent example of the rule of those who wield power through wealth. When he was arrested after a considerable time as a fugitive from justice, Tommy was allegedly given a chummy embrace by the police chief, and allowed the opportunity to have his own press conference. Both Tommy and Suharto crony, Bob Hasan, languished in relative luxury in their respective quarters in jail.

The judge who had previously convicted Tommy was assassinated, and his assassins given life sentences. All awaited to see the fate of Tommy. Did the secret structure of power represented by the remnants of the Suharto regime still prevail? Obviously, within the Suharto support groups, the military were playing a decisive role. Tommy's encounter with the judges during his trial were marked by his insolence and sarcasm. He seemed confident the law could not get him.

When sentencing came, Tommy was absent from court. He was having a bout of diarrhoea, so his doctors reported. The judges gave him fifteen years, *in absentia*, a sentence that many thought was too light. It was the appearance of justice being done. A UN adjudicator who had been sent to Indonesia to assess the quality of the legal process there, concluded, aghast, that the judiciary was the most corrupt he had seen. In Tommy's case, the sentencing *in absentia* would open the way for his lawyers to appeal. And a tedious process would ensue. What price the UN adjudicator's opinion?

# CHAPTER 13

# ANTI-US DISTURBANCES

THE day on which the news broke in Jakarta that the US had begun its strike against Afghanistan (Monday October 8, 2001) saw uneasy calm as police and military strengthened the security measures around the US Embassy. Despite the massing of panzers, the evening saw a trickle of protesters mainly from the FPI, Front for the Defence of Islam, gathering outside the Embassy. According to a report from *detik.com* (October 8, 2001), 500 to 1,000 demonstrators burnt US and British flags, and sang songs to the accompaniment of tambourines.

The next day, the US Embassy was closed. The media had already reported that there were demonstrations in other cities. Elements of the FPI were moving from the provinces towards Jakarta. The situation was complicated by Vice-President Hamzah Haz's support for the extremists, which was counter to Megawati's position. Hamzah Haz was playing a dangerous political game. He hoped, if not to undermine Megawati's position through this support of Islam, at least to acquire popularity with Islamic elements, and hence ease his way to the Presidency.

Demonstrators outside the US Embassy, while not strong in numbers, appeared determined. They tried to break through the barbed wire cordon. Police behind the barricade used water cannon, and tear gas, and fired some warning shots. The demonstrators were not only the FPI, but also Muslim students and the Muslim youth movement (GPI). It was such a representative mix that was ominous. Meanwhile there were calls from the protesters as well as from the Majelis Ulama Indonesia (Indonesian Ulamas' Council) for Indonesia to sever relations with the US.

At the time, the security authorities appeared to have the situation well in hand. Susilo Bambang Yudhoyono was reportedly given the evidence of Osama bin Laden's involvement and Al Qaeda's part in the September 11 events. However, the FPI gave a 72-hour "ultimatum" to government, that if the government did not heed the call to sever relations, then the FPI would appeal to the entire Islamic community in Indonesia to carry out sweeping operations against foreigners, and attack and destroy US interests. The police arrested two protesters on suspicion of being provocateurs. Obviously, there were dirty hands also at work.

The next day, October 10, saw a succession of small demonstrating groups outside the US Embassy. By this time, the FPI from Solo had arrived to join their Jakarta compatriots. These dispersed in the early evening, only to be replaced by a group from the People's Front for Democracy. Meanwhile, a demonstration also took place outside Parliament House. The demonstrators wanted access to the Parliament grounds. Police refused this request, although the protesters had been joined by some Parliament members, among them Ahmad Sumargono. His appeal to Police HQ bore no fruit.

It was gratifying to note how the police stood firm. But amidst the tension, what was significant to was Sumargono's appearance. Sumargono had served as chairman of KISDI, the committee for international solidarity of Islam, one of the less moderate Islamic organisations in Indonesia. One fear was that, as demonstrations met firm police action, frustrated activists could turn to more violent methods of voicing their protests. A bomb threat was reported to the police.

The one prominent factor in the protests was the demand for the government to sever relations with the US. This demand was scoffed at by important government figures. When demonstrators asked the Parliament members who had come to meet them, who would be willing to ask for relations with the US to be severed, only Sumargono raised his hand.

The restlessness in Jakarta continued. Protests were expected to mount, and a massive demonstration was planned for Friday, October 12. Army Chief Endriartono hoped that it would not extend beyond the capital (*Jakarta Post.com* – 11.10.2001). Meanwhile, Megawati was accused of not heeding the interests of Muslims in the country with the world's largest population of Muslims, when deciding on policy with regard to the US attack on Afghanistan. Friday, October 12 came, and it was reported that more than 2,000 individuals had received police permission to demonstrate in front of the US Embassy. At an Istana meeting, Megawati promised to watch closely developments in Afghanistan.

The Jakarta Post reported that thousands of protesters from seven Muslim organisations mounted demonstrations on Friday outside the US Embassy. Although television crews reported that the police used water cannon to disperse the crowds, the authority appeared to have had the situation under control. Crowds melted away before dusk. However, protesters made an earlier attempt to enter the Istana, the official residence of the president. Police hastily set up barricades at the gate. In Makassar, a fast-food outlet was bombed. On Saturday, 13 October, Hizbollah elements from Solo arrived in Jakarta, their intention being to demonstrate probably in front of the US Embassy. This time it was the police who screened them for weapons. In Yogyakarta, a cracker bomb was hurled into a Catholic church by two unidentified persons who fled on a motorcycle. In Mataram in East Indonesia, two German tourists were beaten and kicked. In Lombok, five foreigners were pelted with stones. Vice-President Hamzah Haz urged the US government to stop its attack on Afghanistan. Many voiced approval of this appeal.

Demonstrations started very early in the morning of Sunday October 14. Members of the FPI numbering about 200, gathered before the Jakarta Police HQ. FPI chief Habib Rizique was not among them. He informed *detikcom* when contacted by phone that the demonstration was to demand the release of comrades from the Hizbullah who had been detained at the railway station whence they had arrived from Solo the night before. When the crowd had reached 500, they started throwing stones at the police. They even attempted to gain entry into the police premises. Fortunately, the gates were shut tight.

A short while later, the police freed a portion of the Hizbullah Corps members, who had been languishing at the railway station. However those dozens of would-be demonstrators who happened to be carrying weapons were detained. About a thousand protesters eventually moved off towards FPI's Jakarta HQ. They promised to make for the US Embassy the next day.

Responding to the tensions at a mosque event celebrating the Ascension of the Prophet Muhammed, President Megawati Sukarnoputri declared her abhorrence of terrorism, but said also that no country had the right to summarily attack another in its search for terrorists. The Islamic Youth Movement (GPI) immediately voiced its approval of Megawati's statement. But to other Muslim groups Megawati's fresh view sounded hollow. Some thought that she was playing to the gallery of an Islamic audience, as she was speaking at a mosque. Hamzah Haz had already obtained greater credit with his Muslim followers by calling for a break in relations with the US.

As if challenging the President, the head of the directorate of the Nadlatul Ulama assessed her remarks as good, and proposed that she followed up on them with concrete and practical measures. The Front for the Defence of Islam, appearing to be encouraged by such remarks, threatened to appear before the US Embassy in a protest that had had been going on daily ever since the start of American action against Afghanistan.

But the real focus was on demonstrations in the vicinity of Parliament House. Police used tear gas and water cannon to disperse the mob, apparently consisting mostly of FPI members. So far this was the toughest response from the police mobile brigade (Bri-mob). Media footage showed wounded from among the rioters being attended to, and vehicles with smashed windscreens. The damage had purportedly been done by police elements. The police, on their part, complained of one of their number having to receive several stitches for an injury sustained during the melee. Police also declared that they would take action against those who demonstrated on holidays.

With tension between the police and demonstrators mounting, police action veered towards tougher responses. The ban on demonstrations during public holidays was simply a pretext for unequivocally strong and determined moves on the part of the police. The law enforcers were particularly adamant towards the FPI. But when this extremist group got mauled by police elements, the Laskar Jihad, a brother organisation, declared its indignant support.

# CHAPTER 14

# ASSAULT ON MEGAWATI'S POSITION

IT HAD become clear to Megawati and the TNI that the demonstrations were politically motivated. The Minister for Information and Communication, Sofyan Jalil, declared that the anti-US agitation was not purely an Islamic movement. Indeed, propaganda material had been found even in a mosque, which sought the overthrow of Megawati Sukarnoputri. There were implications that such material could have been produced by third-party elements who hoped to profit from such agitation. Intelligence chief Hendropriyono confirmed the discovery of pamphlets calling for efforts to weaken the leadership of Megawati and her vice-president, Hamzah Haz, who had been busy polishing his Islamic credentials. He postponed a visit to Libya because of unsettled conditions in the Middle East. However, there were occasions when he had differed from Megawati on the government's soft policy towards the US.

So it was surprising that on October 19, Hamzah Haz appealed to thousands of Justice Party (Party Keadilan) supporters at a mosque, urging them not to indulge in further demonstrations. Such manifestations, he said, were having an adverse effect on the economy.

It was uncertain why Hamzah Haz appeared to be changing his mind about anti-US demonstrations, especially after calling for the severing of relations with the US. Perhaps it was because several ministers had spoken of the disastrous effects of such a move as Hamzah had recommended. Leaders of the Nadlatul Ulama and Muhammadiyah also came out in support of maintaining good relations with the United States in order to assure the country of economic recovery.

However, repeated assertions by the TNI, or those who were regarded as highly competent to speak on behalf of the TNI, that the military was fully supportive of Megawati, could have left Hamzah in no doubt that he had better rein in his feelings.

The Justice Party played a more skilful game. It brought out its 10,000 supporters on Friday after prayers, in an anti-US protest, but they behaved as if they were at a picnic. One TV shot showed thousands of Muslim women and girls in a sea of head-to-foot, white-clad participants. They could hardly be seen as a threat to peace, and security forces were at minimum strength. Doves were released at the end of the demonstration.

What appeared to be emerging from such developments was that the TNI was slowly but surely asserting itself as a dominant force to uphold law, order, constitutionality and political stability. It could be likely too that heading towards 2004 were figures with favourable military credentials and upright calibre, and not only excitable Muslim politicians. Significantly, Agus Widjojo ceased to be TNI territorial affairs chief when he was installed as Deputy Speaker of the People's Consultative Assembly (MPR). His predecessor from the military had left this seat vacant to become Minister for Home Affairs.

Meanwhile, Megawati Sukarnoputri gave timely and grave warnings that Indonesia stood the chance of becoming balkanised and enfeebled, if inter-ethnic and religious conflict continued, and territories like Aceh, Riau and West Irian sought to secede, and hence breach the nationalistic principle of the unitary state. If the granting of autonomy to regions encouraged the regions to put ethnic, religious and narrow regional considerations ahead of the nation's interest, then Indonesia would surely disintegrate. Almost like an echo of her words, a brawl broke out on the first day of Parliament among regional representatives, indicating another dimension of regional dissatisfaction.

Many politicians took advantage of the tradition of observing a new president's 100 days in office to launch their criticisms of Megawati. Almost first off the mark was Amien Rais. The promises that had been offered when Megawati first became president had not been fulfilled, he said. But still her achievements could not be judged fairly after only 100 days. Perhaps, magnanimously, one needed to wait for another hundred days to pass before assessing what she and her dream team (her cabinet) had done. University of Indonesia economist Faisal Basri said that not much difference could be discerned between what the Megawati-Hamzah Haz duo did in the first hundred days and the previous administration.

In her first progress report to the MPR, on November 1, Megawati admitted the shortcomings of her brief regime. She tried to deflect criticism of her failure to improve the economic situation by observing that the economic crisis was the result of long-standing weaknesses and the world recession. But her critics had already countered this by noting that she had not even a list of problems and priorities to start off with. Megawati had hoped this would be the end of the criticism in the annual plenary Parliamentary sessions. She tried to get the Assembly to dispense with the yearly session. But law-makers insisted that the ritual of annual meetings be retained. Megawati would continue to be obliged to give an annual accountability speech.

The return of the regional representatives' factions was also a disadvantage for Megawati. Most of the regional representatives would join the Golkar faction in Parliament. Only a few would opt for a merger with PDI-P, for example. Some others would join a Muslim party. But a more serious blow to Megawati's credibility was the murder of Theys Eluay.

# CHAPTER 15

---

# POLITICAL ASSASSINATION
# IN PAPUA

WHILE Indonesia's Parliament was debating the question of direct election to the Presidency, to be effected in 2004, and arriving at an impasse, a tragedy occurred in Irian Jaya. West Papuan leader Theys Eluay was abducted and assassinated. Theys' leadership of the people of Irian Jaya could be traced right back to Suharto's day. But he came into total national prominence when, on November 12, 1999, he proclaimed unilaterally the establishment of the West Papuan State. This he did from his residence in the small town of Sentani, some 30 kilometres from the Irian Jaya capital, Jayapura. From here he also instructed the unfurling of the independence flag "Bintang Kejora" (Morning Star) on December 1, the anniversary of West Papua's independence.

Theys Eluay himself headed the anniversary observances in Jayapura. His view was that the Dutch colonial authority had surrendered sovereignty to the Papuan people on December 1, 1961. Theys met Gus Dur during the latter's presidency, and obtained from him permission to change the name of Irian Jaya to Papua. During Gus Dur's regime, the Papuan leader enjoyed a relatively freer scope of political expression. Gus Dur had prophesied that, should he be overthrown, Papua would seek to detach itself from Indonesia. Theys Eluay himself had once said that he would struggle for his country's independence to the last drop of his blood. That undertaking was sadly fulfilled. The identities of Theys' abductors were not individually known. But the news of the kidnapping was conveyed to Theys' wife by his driver, who said that Theys' vehicle had been stopped by a group of unknown men. Driver and political leader were on their way from Jayapura to Sentani. The driver told Theys' wife that the kidnappers were not Papuans. Then, the driver disappeared, and nothing further was known of him.

Theys Eluay's murder evoked the expected severe reaction, and from varied organisations. For example, the National Solidarity for Papua (SNP) called for the international community (*detik.com* dated November 12, 2001) to urge the Indonesian government to strengthen human rights and create peace. SNP also declared that the killing of Theys showed that Megawati's administration was unable to bring about peace in society. It also showed that there were (subversive) elements that did not want peace in Irian Jaya. SNP also hoped bitterly that the authorities would not try to sweep the case under the carpet, as in Suharto's time.

The political climate in Irian Jaya was complicated by several factors: (a) The society was primitive; (b) It had an immigrant component; (c) Jakarta was suspicious of the intentions of native leaders; (d) autonomy was acceptable to Jakarta, but not independence; (e) Jakarta was fearful Irian Jaya might go the way of East Timor.

Another, and perhaps the most serious condition, was the presence of Yorris Raweyai, a well-known henchman of the Suharto family. He was of mixed Irianese and Chinese descent. He was a friend of Theys Eluay. The Papuan leader did not share the reservations of his other Papuan colleagues about Raweyai's dependability.

Endemic or continual communal unrest in various parts of Indonesia was actually the means of demonstrating that the military was needed. The killing in November 2001 of Theys Eluey, Papuan independence fighter, was allegedly the work of Kopassus – TNI Special Forces.

The TNI, especially certain powerful generals, had well-founded business interests all over Indonesia. Not only were the military determined to protect their profitable interests, they were also eager to preserve power. The TNI received a reprieve when over-active reformist Letjen Agus WK died suddenly and inexplicably.

TNI's powers backed the call for the unitary state of Indonesia. Limited devolution and autonomy was seen as an unfortunate necessity. But a call for independence evoked rage and a bloody response. The annals of East Timor, or rather its most recent history, provided examples of how coarse and cruel the reaction of certain military elements could be.

Not only had the military boldly taken steps in Aceh to preserve their multifarious interests, and in Papua to preempt its economic potential, but the participative action of military elements could be seen in bloody outbreaks of unrest in Maluku and in Sulawesi. For example, although the Christian and Muslim community leaders came to agreement in Maluku, the Laskar Jihad declared their intention to stay. The Laskar Jihad was nothing but the disguised power of Islamic TNI elements.

It might be interesting to speculate on the TNI's flexible operations in Maluku. Was it for the training and deployment of fanatic Muslim do-or-die forces? What was this strategy aimed at? Indonesia's neighbours could be justifiably anxious. Would "divide and rule" and "keep the pot boiling" continue to be the policy of certain TNI pro- anarchy elements, wherever it felt this could be successfully applied?

For such reasons, certain influential parties in the TNI would be willing to keep the whole of Indonesia in ferment. The TNI had also spoken with a forked tongue. Its chief, Admiral Widodo, was reported (in *The Straits Times*, February 15, 2002) as declaring that Indonesia would establish counter-terrorist units to deal with regional security threats. Indeed, there were such units already operating. But scarcely was the saliva dry in his mouth, when explosions rocked Ambon only a day after the peace treaty was signed between Christians and Muslims. After a lull in terrorist acts, there was another later explosion which claimed a few lives. Whose terrorist acts were these? Was the defiant Laskar Jihad responsible? This was to remind the *Serani* (Christians) that Islamists were still around.

Indeed the term *Serani* was (perhaps contemptuously) used by none other than A S Hendropriyono, when he was holding the important position of Minister for Transmigration and Forest Encroachers, and even before he became intelligence chief. At that time, he produced a theory that there was a conspiracy between the GPM (Gereja Protestan Maluku), the RMS (Republik Maluku Selatan) – interpreted by Hendropriyono as Republik Maluku–*Serani* – and Megawati's PDI-P, to grab Maluku for the Christians. For this brilliant piece of theorising, Megawati made – or was forced to make – Hendropriyono her chief of intelligence.

The TNI could not be trusted to crack down completely on Islamic terrorists because of the closeness of certain powerful TNI elements to potential terrorists themselves. George Aditjondro, an expert on negative developments in Indonesia like corruption and extremism (so much so that he has had to seek employment in an Australian university), explained how Laskar Jihad in Maluku had always been headed by Ustadz Ja'afar Umar Thalib. Thalib was a staunch supporter of a neo-Wahabian movement that sought to purge Indonesia of impurities like Christianity and Chinese influences, and turn it into a Muslim state.

Thalib had founded an extremist sect in Yogyakarta, studied in Saudi Arabia and joined the Taliban in Afghanistan. The neo-Wahabi movement triggered the setting up of the Al Irsyad movement in Indonesia. A prominent sponsor of this sect was said to be Fuad Bawazier, finance minister under Suharto. Names of elite personages like Achmad Sumargono and Eggi Sudjana were also associated with Bawazier, as were retired generals Feisal Tanjung and Probowo Subianto (who was alleged to have expressed hatred for Christians and Chinese), besides many others. This had brought Arab-Islamic tinted, ethnically inward-looking political parties and mass organisations (like KISDI or the Indonesian Committee for Solidarity with World Islam) into collusion with militant Jihad.

# CHAPTER 16

---

# HOPE FOR CHANGE: THE HAUNTING OF THREE SUCCESSIVE REGIMES

IN INDONESIA'S recent history, there were political currents and streams that appeared to weave in and out of shady places and underground shelters. Hence, it is difficult to say where the flow was from and where it was going. However, it was occasionally possible to pick out a less shadowy figure floating by, one with more focused outlines. But such a figure would be that of an eager artisan, rather than one of the true creators master-minding Indonesia's chaos.

A retired Ambonese, Brigjen Rustam Kastor, was reputed to be the mind behind Laskar Jihad. His access to current military figures, even up to General Wiranto, was well-known. Although Gus Dur forbade the passage of Laskar Jihad fighters out of Java to Maluku, 10,000 of them were reported to have slithered out of East Java ports, including Surabaya (in Gus Dur's religious stronghold!), probably in Indonesian navy ships.

Rustam Kastor had written a book entitled "Conspiracy of RMS and Christians to destroy Muslims in Ambon and Maluku" – the thesis of which, of course, was vigorously contested. Gus Dur hinted that someone with the initial K to his name was the main provocateur in Ambon. Many thought that Gus Dur was referring to Kivlan Zein, the former Chief of Army (strategic reserve command), Kostrad. Kivlan Zein was ready to lend himself to manipulation by political generals, including Wiranto, who had a bitter feud with Gus Dur. But there was no doubt later that K in fact referred to Brigjen Rustam Kastor (Kivlan Zein was a Mayjen or major-general). But why indeed had Gus Dur to be so mysterious and oblique? Was it because the power of those behind the scenes was too great?

Gus Dur was like ancient Danish king Canute who did not succeed in commanding the tide to hold itself back. The harsh forces of unrest and civil disturbance were washing inexorably over east Indonesia. Rustam Kastor's Indonesian-language book, with its turn-tabling of facts, and other similar publications, received wide publicity. But they continued to trigger ethnic hatred, religious conflict, displaced population shifts, refugee movement, and forced conversions to Islam, even to the extent of compulsory circumcisions. Such happenings were noticed mainly in human rights watch reports and crisis-centre and similar communications, whose distribution and reach were somewhat limited.

Current TNI chief Widodo, although an Admiral and generally moderate in outlook, and a Gus Dur appointee, was relatively helpless. So, when he said he was ready with anti-terrorist bodies, one had to look to Hendropriyono who had scoffed at Singapore's Internal Security regulations, and observe what *his* complexion was like. With such an overlap of several of Islam-oriented extremist bodies in Indonesia, it is hard to believe "Hendro" when he firmly declared that no Al Qaeda network existed in Indonesia. Hendro, however, spoke from the right side of his head when he admitted, at the end of 2001, that Al Qaeda could have been involved in the killings in Poso, South Sulawesi. He was forced to retreat to such a position by the chorus of opposing statements from the US and elsewhere.

Hendropriyono's outlook seemed to be red-and-white, that of a full-blown nationalist. He was suspected of ruthlessly executing Islamic protesters in Lampung, South Sumatra. His current unctuous position was that anybody guilty of breaches of human rights in Timor must be brought to justice. Though, God forbid – he seemed to imply – that any of his general friends should be implicated.

Many of the political elite sincerely or for political reasons favoured Islam. Omar Thalib was detained in Jakarta, but was released soon after. His detention did not prevent him from attending cosy teas with cronies. Nor did it prevent the Indonesian vice-president from visiting him, on the basis of Muslim brotherhood. Thalib's detention was really house arrest.

On Labour Day – May 1, 2002 – a small demonstration was organised by a few labour unions. The most prominent among these unions was that run by radical Eggy Sudjana, namely the Moslem Workers' Brotherhood. Sudjana was an associate of Edi Sasono, a leader in ICMI, the Association of Indonesian Muslim Intellectuals. Although the total membership of such bodies was small compared with Indonesian Muslims as a whole, they were vocal and highly visible, and their leadership ambitious for influential positions. Such were the figures that haunted the corridors of power.

On the high influence of the TNI, President Megawati had been expected to name Jendral Endriartono Sutarto as Chief of Armed Forces, which she did. Actually Endriartono was not Mega's choice. It was Tyasno Sudarto who was her favourite. Neither could Jendral Sutiyoso be Megawati's choice as Jakarta governor. Sutiyoso had been involved in the 1996 attack on the headquarters of the PDI-P, of which Megawati was chief. But officially, at least, Sutiyoso seems to have received Mega's endorsement.

In some quarters there was hope that, if Megawati could get the support of the TNI, some sort of democratic evolution would be more certain. Suharto had every chance in the mid-1980s to pace a transition and succession that would have made the scenario in the nineties politically the right one. Arief Budiman, an Indonesian studies professor teaching at the University of Melbourne, from the beginning stated that Suharto's successor, Habibie, had a sole agenda: To step down. Unfortunately, he was followed by the erratic Gus Dur, and then by the seemingly compliant Megawati Sukarnoputri.

Right through the brief post-Suharto era, influential and powerful elements of the Indonesian government and military extended protection and support to domestic-focused (so far) militant jihad groups. But the military were facing a crisis – human rights trials, public hostility and distrust, insurgency in Aceh and West Papua, civil unrest in Maluku and Sulawesi (which TNI elements helped to foment). There had also been demands for TNI's vast conglomerate holdings to be audited, and gang fights between units engaged in criminal activity (like drugs and prostitution) had occurred.

Still, the military stood powerful. It helped to bring down Gus Dur. Megawati hoped she had TNI's support. But this would be given as long as it suited the military. Indonesia's internal political history in the last half-decade shows the relevance of the adage that there are no permanent friends and no permanent foes. The TNI would side political figures that would bring it advantage. Its support also depended on who was running the TNI. Some analysts even predicted, at the beginning of Megawati's presidency, that she would become the puppet of the TNI.

In mid-2002, the TNI came out with the cry of "return to the 1945 constitution". The fall of Suharto in 1998 saw a fillip given to the democratisation process in Indonesia. At the same time it unleashed discord in several parts of the country. The military also saw its grip on power loosening. A return to the 1945 constitution would give it the opportunity to re-establish itself.

The MPR had before it a tranch of amendments to the 1945 constitution. If agreement could not be reached, those favouring a return to 1945 would carry the day. But in August 2002, religious fundamentalists agitated for the incorporation of traditional Muslim law into the nation's constitution. The Front for the Defence of Islam (FPI) and other radical groups mobilised thousands to agitate for the inclusion of Syariah law in the constitution.

However, Nadlatul Ulama and Muhammadiyah staunchly opposed any change to Clause 29 in the constitution. Amien Rais appeared ready to exercise his duty as MPR Speaker, so that large numbers of MPR members as well as the two massive Muslim organisations, which represented 70 million of the *masyaraka*t, were not in favour of changes to the Pancasila constitution.

# A Burning Question: Was Megawati Capable?

Was Megawati Sukarnoputri fit to carry on as head of state, against the background of her powerlessness? Many were ready to help in an assault on Megawati's position. But it was too early. As long as she remained amenable to the advice of those whose interests she was actually serving, and not be *kepala keras* (hard-headed, stubborn) like Gus Dur, she should survive for the remaining constitutional period of her rule.

Still, some would consider themselves candidates for the presidency in 2004. Two of them were Susilo Bambang Yudhoyono and Agum Gumelar. Both served successively in Abdurrahman Wahid's cabinet. Gus Dur had taken Yudhoyono in because the astute general had been close to Suharto's family as well as to Megawati. Even after Suharto's decline in power, his closeness to the former strongman's family was considered a political plus.

Agum Gumelar, who apparently possessed that same qualification, was quickly chosen by Gus Dur when Yudhoyono distanced himself from the latter. Agum Gumelar then aligned himself with Megawati, and actually contributed to Gus Dur's downfall. Hendropriyono, in the popular imagination, resembled a *wayang* hero like the other two generals. He had together with Agum Gumelar championed Megawati's cause during Suharto's time, and incurred the despot's wrath. But now he emerged from retirement like a legendary figure out of the *Mahabharata*.

In the midst of conflict and lawlessness, a view was briefly mooted that Indonesia was mentally ill. Indonesians were allegedly insensitive to suffering; and there seemed to be an inversion of morality when Amrozi, suspected of being involved in the killing of scores of people, was greeted by police chief Da'i Bachtiar in such a chummy way. It was ugly and scandalous to see Amrozi smiling and joking and waving on Indonesian TV. It was the same unjustness that caused several members of the elite to turn against Megawati when Indonesia lost two small islands to Malaysia in an international court of law.

# CHAPTER 17

# TERRORISM IN BALI

THE most dramatic and shocking event during Megawati's rule was the bombing on October 12, 2002, that ripped through two night clubs in Kuta on the the resort island of Bali. Nearly 200 people were killed and over 300 injured. The horror immediately recalled the September 11 tragedy that hit New York in 2001. The Bali bombings were labelled the worst single terrorist attack since then.

Whether such a dastardly act took the Indonesian authorities completely by surprise requires careful and even profound analysis. Elements of the Indonesian military had, for about three years past, been using Islamic Jihad militia units to ferment unrest – first in Ambon and Maluku, then spreading to Sulawesi and, further east, to Papua New Guinea. There were reports that in the Poso region in Sulawesi, the battles were even used as training events for terrorist components.

It is not certain whether the Bali bombing was the cause of Laskar Jihad forces being de-mobilised. The sudden move, out of sync with the previous havoc caused by the Muslim militia, may have had a surreptitious design. One reason was to disarm suspicion focused on the Jihad after the Bali tragedy occurred. Another was to dodge the mistrust that the manipulators of the Jihad would draw to themselves.

The rogue generals, active and retired, who were involved in the formation and support of the Laskar Jihad, feared the glare of international condemnation, after the Bali bombings. After all, their identities were not so secret. Gus Dur in his time had named their gangster minions as well as hinted at their identities.

Whatever could have been the secret generals' agenda, armed forces chief, Endriartono Sutarto, came out with a clear warning, at the end of October, that Laskar companies should be disbanded. Such armies preparing for war gave the country a bad name for violence, he said. His warning meant that the army was prepared to crack down on extra-institutional, illegal militia groups.

The tragedy of Bali sowed confusion among many in the Indonesian leadership. They had vowed that no terrorist bands existed in Indonesia. How they classified the perpetrators of various bombings that took place in the past was mystifying. These attacks included the end-year 2000 Christmas bombings, the Jakarta foreign exchange bombing, the bombing of the Filipino ambassador's car, and the Atrium Mall bombing in August 2001.

Now Susilo Bambang Yudhoyono asserted that justice would be meted out to the perpetrators, *if there was proof.* This condition was a favoured caution. Others like vice-president Hamzah Haz blew hot and cold. But Megawati Sukarnoputri, ignoring mealy-mouthed protests even from her cabinet members, hastened the passing of emergency laws giving police extended powers of arrest and detention. She could not have done this without urgings from internal quarters as well as pressure from external ones. The Indonesian military, particularly, would be interested in such legislation.

Police investigations proceeded with a speed that surprised foreign observers and gratified all. Sketches of suspects were released. Soon, significant arrests were made. One, Amrozi, confessed to involvement. The chief plotter was identified as Imam Samudra. He was caught in the act of fleeing from Java. The assistance of foreign experts had no doubt expedited the course of investigation. Samudra was alleged to be a member of the Jemaah Islamiyah (JI).

Defence minister Matori Abdul Jalil had already declared that the bombing was positively linked to Al-Qaeda. The JI connection appeared to support this. A suicide bomber was also suspected to be involved, and DNA scientific tests were applied. The Bali bombing was too horrendous and scandalous a terrorist act to allow hidden influences to hinder serious investigations. The detention order against Abu Bakar Bashir was extended. Bashir was alleged to be the spiritual inspiration for Muslim terrorists. Places raided included Muslim boarding schools, although this was done with great discretion, and with as little publicity as possible.

Such caution and sensitivity over Muslim feelings and reactions was advisable in view of important interests. The Laskar Jihad was disbanding itself, but who knew what it was doing underground or behind the scenes? There were other radical groups, like the Front for the Defence of Islam (FPI) and the Indonesian Committee for International Islamic solidarity (KISDI). Members of such organisations had engaged in truculent actions publicly. Thugs *(preman)* were also available for dirty work. Pancasila – Indonesia's political philosophy of five principles: nationalism, democracy, humanism, social justice and monotheism, which had served well in the past – was something such agents merely paid lip-service to.

Moreover, there were several among the top politicians who were looking towards the 2004 parliamentary and presidential elections. They would not want to spoil the Muslim ground for themselves. What had happened to

Megawati and Abdurrahman Wahid in the 1999 presidential elections was a lesson. Gus Dur won and Megawati lost, because of the swing of the Muslim votes, basically through the *poros tengah*, i.e. the central coalition of Muslim forces.

For the same reason, too, Abu Bakar Bashir's strenuous denials about his affiliation with terrorists and terrorist groups delayed his interrogation. No doubt this would have eventually to be connected with the Bali and other bombings. Determined police investigations would put together the pieces of an amazing jigsaw.

# CHAPTER 18

# BOMBS AND THE FAMILY CONNECTION

TIES of blood connected key suspect Amrozi with Ali Imron (who helped in the Bali bombing, but expressed his regret later) and with Imron's step-brother Ali Fauzi. Ali Imron, who was later apprehended in East Kalimantan, as he was about to flee to Malaysia, was Amrozi's brother. Another brother, Ali Gufron alias Mukhlas had a role in the Bali bombing which police were trying to establish. A connection by marriage tied Mukhlas (Ali Gufron) to Hashim Abbas, who was already detained in Singapore. Abbas was Mukhlas' brother-in-law. Family and radicalism contributed to the formation of Amrozi and kin.

Amrozi had been affected by sermons preached by brother Ali Gufron (Mukhlas) and Abu Bakar Bashir. But Amrozi had apparently sat also at the feet of Jafar Umar Thalib, leader of the Laskar Jihad, which had stirred up communal conflict in Maluku and Sulawesi. Imron had allegedly possessed weapons used in the violence in Maluku, which were later secreted and buried. The hidden cache of weapons and ammunition was found in jungle near Imron's village in East Java.

Police fingered Imam Samudra as the Bali bomb plot's mastermind. Yet he was said to be subordinate to the head of the operation – none other than Ali Gufron aka Mukhlas. Imam Samudra was the expert at making and working the bombs, but Amrozi's brother Mukhlas was the boss. An important connection was revealed when investigations found that money for the operation came from a certain Malaysian called Wan Min, whom the Malaysians already had in custody. The money came from a jewellery heist. So many lives and millions of dollars had been lost, and the cost to the perpetrators was a mere US$35,000.

One question arising was how many more family-centred cells like the one to which Amrozi belonged, existed in Indonesia? What sort of cross-national or international connection did they have? What sort of connection did such cells have with Laskar Jihad, which had now been ordered to be quiescent? What about the generals and lower orders who moved the Laskar Jihad, and even inhabited it?

Was the emotional pull of family exploited to make it the psychological centre of a much wider network? Certainly beyond the family, new names with significant roles were distributed over a larger mesh. One Syafullah, a Yemeni, was believed to have coordinated the bombing with Mukhlas who had authority over Imam Samudra. Syafullah led to Al Qaeda. Syafullah gave the inputs to Mukhlas, the Jemaah Islamiah operative who managed Samudra the technical expert. Such an evil affiliation led the gang of half a dozen or so who took part in the Bali attack.

Apart from the Malaysian money-man Wan Min, another Malaysian, Zubair, allegedly surveyed and mapped the targeted site. Interestingly, a man named Syawal, who was said to be intricately involved in the planning of the Bali attack, had been an instructor in a training camp in the region of Poso in Sulawesi where the Laskar Jihad had instigated incidents of unrest. What was the link, if any, between Al Qaeda, which had a connection with the camp, and Laskar Jihad, which was operating in the vicinity? The net was getting wider and the species of fish more interesting.

Yet, despite the terrorist family's overseas connections, the influence of terrorist actions appeared constrained by the limitations of the small group. The damage done was terribly harmful. But the government could draw some relief from the knowledge that the larger Islamic community shrank from an association with the anti-social activities of the extremists.

At the same time, the international features of the attack on Bali seemed to have brought a focus on domestic terrorism like the Christmas Eve 2000 bombings. Imam Samudra confessed to knowing about the Christmas bombings. Police continued to question Samudra and others about various bombings that took place also in 2001. These bombings as well as some that occurred in the Suharto era show that the readiness to resort to terrorist action was more widespread and deep-rooted than suspected previously. Moreover the homegrown variety of terrorism had elements of rogue official sanction behind it.

A later revelation came from Singapore's Home Affairs minister in November 2003. Speaking at a security conference in Hawaii, Minister Wong Kan Seng pointed out that the current turn of events showed that young sons of Jemaah Islamiyah militants were being inducted into jihad. This came to light as a result of recent security operations in Pakistan. Al Qaeda and the JI were ready to bestow their horrifying legacy on a new generation of terrorists. The Hawaii conference called for united zeal in battling terrorism.

International cooperation in the Bali investigations was significant. There were (internal) difficulties in dealing with terrorism emanating from the Laskar Jihad. But it was acknowledged by the Indonesian side itself that investigation into the Bali blasts would have been stymied had it not been for assistance rendered by foreign experts. Although Gen I Made Mangku Pastika, the Balinese chief of investigations, pursued his task with grim zeal, high-tech approaches, new investigation techniques and sophisticated forensics helped immensely in revealing culprits and their basic network. The credibility of the police received a much-needed boost.

Reconstructions of the blasts gave a helpful, three-dimensional picture of the crime scene. Explosives experts had provided clues very early in the investigations. Forensic tests led to a vehicle connected with the bombings. This in turn led to Amrozi. Accurate tracing of mobile signals led to Mukhlas. Indonesian investigators had become acquainted with highly sophisticated techniques that could be used in future investigations. Hopefully, bombings that occurred after Bali (like the McDonalds in Makassar), and those that had happened before (like the year 2000 Christmas Eve blasts), could be more expertly looked at.

The Bali bombings investigations showed a thoroughness and extended patience that had not previously characterised the effort or style or technique of local authorities. Eight Bali suspects were flown under heavily armed escort to Solo in Central Java. Here they were to reconstruct meetings allegedly held to plan the Bali bombings. After this they were to be taken to Surabaya where, some of the accused claimed, the explosives were bought. Surabaya's Internet cafes were also allegedly the favourite haunts of key suspect Samudra.

In east Java, the suspects also re-enacted the meeting, which took place at their home in Tenggulun, previous to the Bali attack. It had been reported earlier that, in about mid-December, local police had uncovered one tonne of potassium chlorate in Tenggulun. It was deduced to be part of the huge cache of chemicals Amrozi had admitted to buying in preparation for attacks like the Bali bombing.

One positive trend that emerged from the fight against terrorism concerned the Indonesian police establishment. Now separated from the TNI, the police had acquired greater self-confidence (while acknowledging the external help it received) in the way it performed its investigative functions.

# CHAPTER 19

# SEQUEL TO THE BALI BOMBINGS

AN interesting aspect of the Bali bombing was the greater light it threw on terrorism in Indonesia. Earlier, responding to the international clamour for action against terrorism, Indonesian officials took the view that no such activities occurred in Indonesia. Laskar Jihad activities in Maluku and then Sulawesi did not seem to be regarded as terrorist acts. Jafar Umar Thalib, Laskar Jihad's founder, knew Al Qaeda operatives and had met them, but rejected their overtures for cooperation. But for whom, and by whose permission, was the training camp in Poso established by agents close to Al Qaeda?

The US criticised Indonesia for its delay in acting against terrorists on home ground, and in failing to take action against those accused by Malaysia and Singapore of having terrorist links. But action against Jemaah Islamiyah, which had been formed by Ali Murtopo as a trap for radical Muslims, and which had indeed caught Abu Bakar Bashir, was difficult to knock out.

For the first part of 2002, while Malaysia and Singapore had detained Islamic militants, Indonesia was shuffling its feet. Perhaps it was doing so in the expectation of getting aid from foreign donors, especially the US, to improve the military capability of the TNI. But such assistance was not forthcoming, and even Abu Bakar Bashir had yet to be arrested. On May 4, Megawati arrested Jafar Umar Thalib, head of the Laskar Jihad. Thalib had obviously gone beyond the bounds of propriety by preaching for the extermination of former president Sukarno's family!

During Thalib's incarceration in Surabaya, vice-president Hamzah Haz paid him a friendly visit. Obviously such a politician as Haz had to take every opportunity of wooing constituents. This was the problem of instituting an anti-terrorist campaign against Muslims – the political backlash.

One important minister who, from the first, blamed Al Qaeda for the Bali bombing was Matori Abdul Jalil. Indonesian authorities had maintained that it did not have the emergency laws to take effective measures against its domestic terrorists. One minister had even jeered at Singapore's security preservation legislation. But within a week of the Bali bombings, Megawati Sukarnoputri had signed two new laws giving authority for detention without trial, and for the death penalty for acts of terrorism. Abu Bakar Bashir was detained for questioning.

It was immediately after the Bali tragedy that some person or some authority gave the order for the Laskar Jihad (LJ) to be disbanded. Obedience to such instructions appeared prompt. The LJ headquarters in Jogjakarta were closed down; LJ members stopped collecting money at road junctions; and the LJ website was shut down. Large contingents of Laskar Jihad militia returned to Java from Maluku.

Vice-president Hamzah Haz wanted the LJ to de-mobilise to reduce tensions after Bali. Those de-mobbed could still contribute to local medical and welfare activities. It would appear that suddenly peace had come to erstwhile troubled regions, and there was no need for the activities of armed militia. Yet only five months previously, Jafar Umar Thalib had issued a declaration of war against Christians and those who supported them, including the regional authority.

Were the military and political elite elements, who wanted to use the Laskar Jihad for their own purposes, finding Jafar Umar Thalib a nuisance, and the Laskar Jihad an embarrassment after Bali? Umar Thalib's truculent declaration triggered a sharper conflict between supporters of the Laskar Jihad and those who noted its activities with regret and, indeed, with alarm. The Bali tragedy could not but have given a more persuasive force to the arguments of those highly critical of the Laskar Jihad, and who wre concerned about international condemnation and the blight on Indonesia's overseas image.

Yet, the Laskar Jihad's protectors were working full-time on its behalf. Although Jafar Umar Thalib could receive a seven-year sentence for preaching serious discord and urging murder, the *prosecutors*, not his defence lawyers, pleaded for leniency. They asked for a one-year sentence on framing a lower charge. The explanation for the plea for leniency was the fact that Thalib had never been imprisoned before, and his courteous behaviour in court. Even such a plea was unacceptable to Jafar Umar Thalib. He said that he could not admit any guilt at all. In his view, Muslims and Christians could never stop fighting.

Such a kind-hearted outlook towards those who were notorious for acts of religious extremism could be compared with the kindness and consideration shown towards convicted criminals with powerful connections. Bob Hasan, an old friend of Suharto and now serving time for corruption, was reported to have frequently been given time off to see his private doctor.

There were also conjectures that Tommy Suharto, imprisoned for murder was being given special treatment, including furloughs, like Bob Hasan.

Maybe armed forces commander Endriartono Sutarto had his tongue firmly in his cheek. In an avuncular manner, he shook a finger at militias belonging to organisations like Nadlatul Ulama, and asked them to disband. He said they should emulate the good behaviour of the militant Defenders of Islam Front (FPI) which had suspended its paramilitary wing.

The general advised that such militias which had been formed by religious organisations like the NU and Muhammadiyah should be de-activated. They were no longer relevant in the environment of *reformasi*! By the same token, there was no need for the FPI, for example, to try (as was alleged) to collect protection money from owners of entertainment night-spots.

Solahudin Majid, a human rights official, declared that the existence of paramilitary gangs was a negative influence on democracy. He said that he believed that the FPI was dissolved because its sponsors were afraid they might become targets of the global war on terrorism. Just as enlightening was the view of a prominent Muslim NU scholar that the FPI had dissolved itself, because it had lost the political protection from generals. It was a pity that the two prominent gentlemen did not mention who the sponsors and generals were, although they sounded as if they knew them.

If a further illustration of this sort of spirit were needed, the deadly bombing of a McDonald's restaurant in Makassar provided it. Apparently, Suryadi, one of the suspects in the Makassar bombing, was a friend of Imam Samudra, one of the chief figures in the Bali bombing. Although at least some of the Makassar suspects belonged to an extremist organisation, the Laskar Jundullah, references to such membership were hushed up.

With regard to the perpetrators of the Bali bombing, Imam Samudra, who planned the attack, was sentenced to death. Mukhlas (aka Ali Gufron) was accused of masterminding the attack. Ali Imron, convicted of assembling the principal explosive, was sentenced to life imprisonment. It was Imron's quiet and submissive behaviour, and his adjudgedly sincere expression of remorse, that earned him the lesser sentence.'Amrozi, the smiling bomber, received the death penalty. Abu Bakar Bashir received a sentence of four years in jail. He had been accused of subversion, but was acquitted of being the spiritual leader of Jemaah Islamiyah.

# The Saga Of Abu Bakar Bashir

The story of Abu Bakar Bashir was a real saga. Detained by the Indonesian authorities since October 2002, he was suspected of involvement in the Christmas Eve 2000 bombings, and also of plotting to assassinate President Megawati and of planning to blow up the national Istiqlal Mosque in Jakarta. The questioning of a JI suspect caught in Singapore elicited incriminating information about Abu Bakar Bashir, and also about his association with two of the Bali bombers.

This frail-looking, grandfatherly cleric had always been outspoken in his admiration for Osama bin Laden. Like Laskar Jihad's Jafar Umar Thalib, Bashir professed the beliefs of the puritanical Wahabi sect of Islam. He "held court" in a *pesantren* in Ngruki in Solo. He began to feel that he was unassailable. He defied police investigation, claiming to be medically unfit. When he appeared able to be questioned, he set conditions – one of which was for police to apologise for detaining him!

Yet Singapore and Malaysian police and intelligence authorities alleged Bashir to be closely connected to Jemaah Islamiyah and Al Qaeda. Bashir dared to make impossible demands such as being allowed to confront Omar al-Faruq who was in detention in the US. Omar al-Faruq had accused Bashir of being involved in terrorism in Indonesia. In Indonesia's current circumstances of varied conflict and rising power of minority yet influential radicalism, Bashir felt protected by his profession of Islamic faith.

He was known to head the Indonesian Mujahidin Council (MMI). The government itself was wary about arresting and charging Bashir. This cautious, ambivalent attitude may be regarded as encouraging to Al Qaeda and Jemaah Islamiyah. Western governments were concerned. The daring Abu Bakar Bashir promised to sue the Singapore government for more than $100 million, because of Singapore's accusations that Bashir was linked with Al Qaeda through the Jemaah Islamiyah.

Despite evidence from both Malaysia and Singapore pointing to Bashir's involvement with the JI, of which he was alleged to have been its one-time head, the court before which Bashir appeared decided it could find no evidence of this. Even an allegation that he had headed a plot to assassinate President Megawati was discounted. Bashir was convicted of only being involved in a treasonous plot against the Indonesian government. He was sentenced to four years' imprisonment.

But Bashir was not yet in the clear.

Fresh charges against him came just days before the new administration of President-elect Susilo Bambang Yudhoyono was sworn into power. Dr Yudhoyono is expected to take a tougher stand on terrorism. State prosecutors filed charges accusing the 66-year-old preacher of being party to a "sinister conspiracy" to bomb nightclubs in Bali in 2002, the country's worst terrorist attack. At the time of writing, Bashir faces a jail term of 20 years to life if convicted. Bashir was also accused of plotting the 2003 Marriott hotel bombing that killed 12 people. He may face the death penalty for that incident under Indonesia's tough new anti-terrorism laws.

Former attorney-general Marzuki Darusman told The Sunday Times: "The prosecutors are drawing on the same evidence against Bashir but using a different legal basis to pin him down. It is a victory of sorts after having had

their case stalled by the Constitutional Court."
(Source: *The Sunday Times,* October 17, 2004)

CHAPTER 20

# RELATIONS WITH SINGAPORE

PROBABLY the main sticking point in Indonesia's dealings with Singapore was its refusal over decades to sign an extradition agreement with Indonesia. Another was the difference in Singapore's representation of trade with Indonesia, as compared with Indonesia's relevant trade statistics. There were also grumbles over illicit mining for sand intended for Singapore. But this was more a regional complaint from Riau.

For the grouses, Singapore produced the usual, but to the Indonesians, repulsive, response. Namely, that it was plain economics that caused Indonesian capitalists to flee Indonesia. And that it was not the Singapore government, but operators mining the sand who obtained permits to do so. Were the differences in trade statistics simply the result of each country having its own angle of vision?

Although newspaper headlines proclaimed that Prime Minister Goh Chok Tong's Jakarta mid-December 2002 visit paved the way to better relations, old irritations still remained to surface on future occasions. Actually the visit was to try for better cooperation in the fight against terrorism. Megawati admitted that the threat was very grave. Goh said that his discussion with Megawati had been "quite deep". It may be interesting to speculate if it was she who informed Goh that the roots of terrorism went back to the Darul Islam rebellion.

Did Megawati tell Goh that it was Ali Murtopo who in 1977 designed a sting operation against Darul Islam? He persuaded some Darul Islam operatives to surface as Jemaah Islamiyah in a purportedly anti-communist move. Instead Indonesian security arrested nearly 200 Darul Islam/Jemaah Islamiyah members. Some senior military continued their contacts with JI. Did they do it right up to the time of the Bali bombing?

For months up to the time of the Bali bombings, most important Indonesian officials were strenuously denying the existence of any terrorism at all in Indonesia. In early 2002, when Senior Minister Lee Kuan Yew declared that Muslim extremist leaders were roaming freely in Indonesia, Hamzah Haz wanted the Singapore government to clarify Lee's statement. The Indonesian foreign ministry summoned a representative of Singapore's embassy, to express the Indonesian government's displeasure.

Now at least, with the Goh-Megawati meeting in Bogor, there was a breakthrough in common understanding, although it was not complete. Indonesians were still saying that they could not follow Singapore in adopting, for example, such draconian legislation as detention without trial. For this was not part of the *reformasi* Indonesia wanted to adopt.

With Goh Chok Tong's visit, the effort to improve economic opportunity for Indonesia was also on the cards. The $1.2 billion dollar link-up of Singapore's ST Telemedia and Indonesian PT Indosat in 2002 was an exemplary achievement. But some 200 Indosat workers staged a protest on the day of an important shareholders' meeting.

Were they a rent-a-crowd group that would not be difficult to bring together at that time? But the "benchmark" of how a transparent and profitable business deal could be achieved elicited political complaints. Were such grouses mostly triggered by envy? At the same time politicians with an eye to the 2004 elections jumped on the "nationalist" bandwagon. These wanted the Indosat sale to be either to a local consortium or to a Malaysian concern. Politicians with vested interests were ready to hurt the country's economic chances by spoiling an exemplary economic deal. Were the vested interests purely political?

The Singapore prime minister's statement that Singapore Airlines was offering specially cheap tickets to Bali was intended to restore tourism to the erstwhile paradise island. Mr Goh reiterated: "Bali is a safe place to go." It might be recalled that Singapore's prime minister had visited Indonesia two years previously. He had brought with him a promising package of US$1.5 billion of investments. Shortly after this, the Christmas Eve 2000 bombings took place. It was as if some malignant force or forces were defying attempts to jack up Indonesia's economy. Those plotting such trouble did not touch Bali except for threatening growls. It was two years later in October that Bali was tragically hit.

Singapore has tried to respond to Indonesia's call for financial assistance and investment. But Singapore's response has always been based on a rational look at mutual benefit and understanding. For example, Goh Chok Tong's package could not be opened in 2000, because the Indonesian side could not produce a balance, as was originally conceived. This led to hard feelings on the Indonesian side, which had placed high hopes on the Singapore offer. Now that Megawati and Chok Tong had got together to talk not only security but also economics, the wicked minds that brewed the Christmas bombings must have gone into high gear to seek retaliation.

The question of long-term relations between Indonesia and Singapore remained, even while Indonesia examined her problems. The first thing would be for each side to jettison false conceptions and stereotypes of the other.

Singaporeans also needed to shed their propensity for a purely rational approach to what the Indonesians needed. Habibie tried to do this for his country. And he fell – rapidly.

The example of the Soviet Union as it was in the throes of collapse should provide a useful lesson. Simply put, people rejected Gorbachev, because he wanted to hurry reform. In the same way, Habibie and Gus Dur wanted *reformasi* and *demokrasie* when the application of such premature concepts would have plunged Indonesia into further chaos.

Indonesia had relatively prospered (for three decades!) under a centralised system, headed by the military, at the behest of a single individual.

# CHAPTER 21

# MEGAWATI'S POLITICAL CHALLENGES

GENERAL disappointment with Mega's rule crept in, perhaps more obviously, at the turn of the year 2002 – 2003. The S$1.2 billion stake acquired by Singapore's STT in Indonesia's Indosat was economically a plus for Indonesia, and a pointer towards foreign investment growth. Yet workers started protesting against the deal. This could have been a quick knee-jerk reaction of Indonesian workers, but it also may have been a symptom of political manipulation.

In fact, some Indonesian law-makers already threatened to urge an enquiry into the merger. They would have had a small rationale for such action, for the circumstances of the STT-Indosat combine were transparent enough. But a minority of legislators wanted to make trouble for Megawati. Abdurrahman Wahid accused some members of Megawati's PDI-P of receiving bribes to support STT's proposal.

Other politicians suggested it was a sell-out to Singapore interests. They contended that selling such a large share to Singapore presented long-term threats to Indonesia. Both Vice-President Hamzah Haz and Parliament Deputy Speaker A M Fatwa questioned whether the sale of a strategic asset like Indosat exposed Indonesia to security risks. Still others questioned the policy itself of privatisation to serve budgetary needs.

Obviously, those politicians in opposition to Megawati, or some with their own political agenda connected with the 2004 elections, were storing up ammunition with which to storm the Megawati redoubt. Such a vote-catching effort might have had a political effect, but moves made simply to advance personal interests would at the same time make investors wary, if it did not turn them away completely.

In the regions and in Java too, sporadic student and youth organisations were demonstrating against Megawati for the rise in fuel, electricity and telephone charges. They alleged that such increases would trigger food prices and augment the people's misery. They argued that Megawati had been unable to diminish the people's suffering. They railed against Megawati's ineffective rule, and for effect, they included as inefficient her sale of government assets to foreigners.

Not only were workers, students and youth organisations irked by the joist in fuel prices. Indonesian companies were threatening not to pay their taxes. They cited increasing costs as the reason for their threatened action. Companies complained that their survival was at stake. Wages had doubled in the last three years. Now workers were demanding more because of fuel and electricity price hikes.

What would be more embarrassing for Megawati would be a ganging up of workers and their employers to make a joint protest against the electricity and fuel price hikes. Protests over higher prices in May 1998 escalated into bitter rioting which was costly in lives. This eventually brought down Suharto. One of the figures apparently applauding a joint labour employer demonstration was wealthy businessman Sofyan Wanandi. Sofyan featured in a brief past scenario where he was accused of being a terrorist, although the charge was later dropped. But more regularly, his role was head of an economic recovery commission.

Amid such restlessness, there were calls for Megawati to step down. This sounded like a grim re-play of Abdurrahman Wahid's time when it was Megawati who denounced Gus Dur. In the evolving game-play, it was Gus Dur's turn to serve. He accused Megawati's party members of corruption. But, true to his style, Gus Dur refused to name the accused and to quote chapter and verse. Apparently the former president wanted his enemies to stew in their own juice, before completing his revelations. This smacked of deliberate gamesmanship, for the ultimate target would be Megawati herself. It was interesting that political parties were generally trying to court public favour by supporting student protests. Even Gus Dur's National Awakening Party said it was right for strikes to be called in protest against the price hikes. But Golkar maintained its cool. Golkar chief Akbar Tandjung advised that strikes would only cause people to suffer more. Did this show Golkar was trying to position itself unctuously on the government's side? The crucial question, as always, would be: Where would the military ultimately lean?

Amid all the protests and demonstrations against the price hikes, Megawati arose to defend her decision to raise fuel and power prices. She was addressing a rally of tens of thousands of PDI-P supporters in Bali. She said she wanted to reduce foreign debt, and in this way free the economy. In the past, she averred, it had been popular for the government to heavily subvent oil and fuel prices. But this had in fact destroyed the nation's economic foundation.

Her arguments did little to stem the tide of unrest. Calls for more demonstrations began to spread, with the latest coming from a student meeting held at Muhammadiyah headquarters. Surprisingly, even the PDI-P faction in Parliament added to the mounting pressure on Megawati to defer the price hike policy or loosen its application, in response to the people's suffering.

Indonesia's lawmakers did not want to risk initiatives that would threaten their political status or individual interests. A large group of them petitioned the government, to show the public where many political parties and members of parliament stood. As a result of calls for Megawati to step down, there was talk of putting together a "national presidium" to replace the current president/vice-president leadership.

MPR Speaker Amien Rais sounded out a view that the government should be prepared for a constitutional removal, if it refused to hearken to cross-country street protests. Coordinating Political and Security Affairs Minister Susilo Bambang Yudhoyono warned that attempts to bring down the government would be met with a response. Would the TNI step in?

Amien Rais went a step further. Apparently supported by the MPR of which he was chairman or house leader, he asked for a meeting with Megawati herself. Such a political ploy was lambasted in a *Media Indonesia* editorial on January 15, 2003. But even to an ordinary observer Amien Rais was attempting an all-round upmanship.

If Megawati met Amien and listened to his arguments as representative of the upper house of parliament, Amien would score. If Amien were sent away empty, he would still resort to his agitation in the media. One way or another he would appear a people's champion, he hoped. In the end Megawati replied and said that she would meet all MPR members. But the TNI specifically mentioned Amien Rais in its warning against unrest.

The TNI stated that street protests were acceptable, but attempts to topple President Megawati Sukarnoputri would be tackled head-on. The TNI must have noted that protesters in Jakarta had twice succeeded in breaking down the gates blocking access into parliament grounds.

But even after the TNI caution, police had to fire warning shots. Demonstrators had attacked the Sulawesi ofice of the PDI-P, and damaged it. They claimed that they had been pelted with rocks from the inside of the office. Things were obviously getting rougher. The TNI was saying that it did not favour unconstitutional means to overturn the rightful authority, which was fair enough. Why not wait till the 2004 elections? Yet there were rumours in Jakarta that, if Megawati did not play her cards successfully, the military could be poised for a coup. But such rumours had become rife since Habibie's time.

The disposition of political forces, just after the start of 2003, showed an interesting change. Such were the circumstances that would persuade the military to wait and see, unless the security situation became dangerous. The Golkar Party was showing surprising resilience. Everybody had said Golkar was going down the drain, because of its past association with Suharto, and also because its chief, Akbar Tandjung, had been convicted of corruption.

But in the regions, many Golkar leaders and executives were elected as governor and regent or mayor. In some cases, they displaced PDI-P holders or contenders. Golkar was said to be strengthening its unity and solidarity. In contrast, the leadership of the PDI-P appeared to have split into three camps, with one at least disgruntled over the appearance of the party not fighting for the poor. Megawati's party was reportedly split from the PDI-P into PDI Perjuangan Rakyat, the Nationalist Bung Karno Party and the Indonesian Motherland Party. Other parties had also suffered splits. PKB, for example had two rival segments, one headed by Matori Abdul Jalil, and the other by Alwi Shihab. Jalil broke off from Gus Dur and joined Megawati, while Shihab stayed loyal to Gus Dur. Vice-President Hamzah Haz's PPP split into PPP and the United Development Party of Reform. Amien Rais' PAN had already earlier suffered division with the walkout of economist Faisal Basri and politician Bara Hasibuan.

The military would not, in the long run, be so eager to support such vehicles as Megawati's weakened PDI-P. A renewed Golkar would more likely be the military's choice for partnership, if it were through the constitutional process, namely the Elections. Perhaps it was because of such far-sighted optimism that Golkar had unctuously stated that strikes and such action would only end up with the people suffering more. The Golkar Party was seen as being more accommodating on sensitive issues, making its public image more amiable. But Golkar would not have been able to go it alone. Logically they would need to look towards the PDI-P for partnership.

It would have been too early at the beginning of 2003 to make a prediction about Golkar's complete re-vitalisation. And it would also be too early to say if, as had been rumoured, a powerful potential icon like the Jogja governor (hereditary prince Hamengku Buwono) might emerge as a universally acclaimed candidate. But any potential presidential candidate might do worse than look at the Golkar party as an instrument of political aspiration.

# The Aceh Problem : Another Thorn In Mega's Side?

The crisis-ridden area having a critical effect on the 2004 elections would be Aceh. One province that would have jettisoned Pancasila, if it could, was Aceh. In this most important area of long-lasting conflict between government forces and rebels, in Aceh, battles continued. In the year 2000, Abdurrahman Wahid initiated a truce with the separatists. The agreement was signed in Davos, Switzerland, by Hassan Wirajuda, at that time Indonesia's permanent representative at UN. A hail of internal criticism greeted Gus Dur's initiative.

Aceh bombings and assassinations continued. Just before Megawati's brief visit to Aceh took place, for talks with community leaders on September 9, 2001 Rector Dayan Dawood of Syiah Kuala University in Banda Aceh was murdered. Immediately after Megawati left, the community leaders were kidnapped and held for 24 hours by members of the Free Aceh Movement (GAM).

By 2002, the Henry Dunant Centre for humanitarian dialogue had been attempting to mediate between TNI and GAM for over two years. They had held eight meetings since Gus Dur's time. But in June 2002, the commander of the Aceh operational command asked the Dunant centre to make its activities more transparent. It appeared that the centre had called together at its secretariat in Banda Aceh a number of self-help social organisations. And it did not inform the military about it. The centre replied that it was seeking input for an all-inclusive dialogue between the Indonesian government and GAM. It had not gone beyond its agreed functions.

In July 2002, the Henri Dunant Centre was asked to quit Aceh. The allegation was that the Centre had failed as facilitator, and was sympathetic to GAM. Wirayuda, who had by this time become foreign minister, hinted that the HDC had exceeded its mandate. GAM was branded as "terrorist".

August 17 was Indonesia's independence day and celebrations were greeted in Aceh by widespread rioting, bank bombings, and the burning of as many as 60 schools. Many casualties and four deaths were caused. On the same national day, Megawati apologised to the six million people of Aceh and Irian Jaya for past years of human rights violations. But she added that although a special autonomous structure governing the two provinces would be desirable, independence was out of the question.

While the TNI was watching the unfolding of peace negotiations with an eagle eye, GAM was also suspicious. It was difficult to bring peace to a region that had seen fighting between separatist rebels and the Indonesian government for 26 years. But the Henry Dunant centre announced that an agreement would be signed in Geneva on December 9. This accord would offer more autonomy to 4 million Acehnese, and elections to Aceh's provincial legislature and administration. International as well as Indonesian monitors would check on how the peace deal was being observed.

Still it was gloomily predicted that the rebels held the key to lasting peace. Even as Indonesian government and GAM representatives were heading for Geneva where both sides would pledge to cease hostilities, a barge carrying explosives was seized by the Indonesian navy. Rebels also shot a soldier who refused to surrender.

GAM had not given up the idea of secession. It was not certain that the Henry Dunant Centre had successfully negotiated an accord with Hasan di Tiro. Thus it was only a cessation of hostilities that had resulted. Even then GAM representatives expressed reservations that monitoring of the accord would be complete. In Banda Aceh, 5000 people gathered at the main mosque to pray. On previous national-provincial occasions hundreds of thousands had gathered ostensibly for the same reason.

Since May 2003, the Indonesian government has launched an integrated military operation to eliminate GAM rebels.

# Will The Military Stage A Comeback?

The military has dominated the Indonesian political scene almost from the very beginning of Indonesia's statehood or existence as a national entity. It moved into a position of quiet authority under Megawati's aegis. At about the time of the Bali bombing, Megawati's popularity was waning. Although very soon after the tragedy, she displayed firmness in exercising her prerogative to initiate special powers for the police, she was generally accused of indecisiveness and a want of leadership skills. In the very fluid political circumstances that prevailed, and with the military yearning for its former saturating influence, a good question would be, what would happen in 2004?

The fact remained that those who resented the military's power were the political, official and business elite. It could not be imagined that the *rakyat*, those who had at one time screamingly supported Megawati, the groundswell in the *poros tengah*, the followers of Amien Rais and the faithful in the Nadlatul Ulama cared deeply one way or the other whether ABRI still wanted to "*masok desa*".

In 2002, the Indonesian president had gone to Papua during the Christmas season, and joined in the singing during celebrations. She also inaugurated a liquefied natural gas project, which with other rich on-going projects could bring wealth to Papua. An autonomous plan was being prepared, like the one offered Aceh.

However the Acehnese were cynical of central government intentions. So were the Papuans, who were yet sorrowing over what they regarded as the assassination of their leader Theys Eluay one year back. Still the quietly voiced military option in case Papua or Aceh chose the way of separatists hung over them like the sword of Damocles.

There were many possible winning cards in the Indonesian political pack. At the beginning of the year 2003, in a still very fluid situation, observers could not pre-empt their choice of who would spring from the bundle. As the year proceeded names of potential candidates began to crop up. At first Muslim scholar Nurcholish Madjid was ahead in the popularity stakes. But later, names appearing were: former TNI chief Wiranto, former army special forces (Kopassus) commander Prabowo Subianto, who had married and divorced Suharto's daughter, media boss Surya Paloh, and Yogyakarta Sultan Hamengku Buwono X. Akbar Tandjung, Golkar chief, who was awaiting an appeal against a conviction for corruption, would probably try his chance. Of course,

Megawati had not discarded her own participation.

It would be interesting to speculate how much the shadow of Suharto would hang over the events in the coming competition for the presidency. Both Habibie and Gus Dur were brought to realise the respective nature of their hubris, and were forced to give up their presidencies, because they lacked the support of the military elements and the surrogates of the Suharto *Orde Baru* (New Order).

On the other hand, violence and disorder in the Indonesian archipelago's periphery – patently engineered, by segments of the military, even during Megawati's regime – sought to demonstrate how much the strong arm of the military's influence in government was needed.

The Bali bombing made the military elements, responsible for internecine conflict, call off their Muslim jihad-ist militia. The military did not want their own hounds to be identified with Islamic Jemaah Islamiyah and Al Qaeda terrorists. This was why in the early confusion after the Bali bombing some top figures, even like Susilo Bambang Yudhoyono, in Indonesia's leadership appeared confused.

# CHAPTER 22

# MEGAWATI'S ADMINISTRATIVE CHALLENGES

T HE serious widespread protests against the fuel and related hikes showed a basic failure in Megawati's administrative management and control. Instead of seeking a clearer political consensus, Megawati still continued to think in terms of presidential decree. So, in fact, did an inept parliament.

The price hikes had actually been debated and approved within the ambit of the Budget for year 2003. Why then did so many members of parliament join in the protests against the hikes? An innocent observer may be forgiven for concluding that many Indonesian members of parliament were not too attentive to what was going on in their area of responsibility; or were knaves who had gone into parliament for a free ride to enjoy the perks of their station. Or could it have been that the executive misled parliament, or did not inform the House adequately? And where did presidential responsibility lie between all these traps?

The real problem was that three decades of despotic rule had left a habit of administrative fiat that was difficult to shake off. Now it had become necessary for a budding democracy to make decisions and policies based on a political consensus reflecting national ownership. If they had to suffer the consequences of administrative action, people wanted transparency, so that they could understand what it was all about, before decisions were made.

The problem for the government was that there was not merely one crisis – but many crises – confronting it. It was not surprising that both government and the legislature found the situation mind-boggling. Corporate restructuring and privatisation were only two major government measures impeded by public misunderstanding and mindless xenophobia. And yet they were crucial for sustaining external confidence and economic recovery. These and other critical policies had first to be sold to the people through effective media management and the use of social education outlets.

Where the *rakyat* were concerned, a very small percentage of them read newspapers. There had to be a significant fallback on radio and television. It would also be the responsibility of parliament and its members to educate themselves to the overall understanding of the economic necessities of policy measures, and convey such understanding to party followers. But MPs tended to ask to be given details, which might require high technical understanding. Above all, national interest should over-ride narrow political interests.

The aim to cooperate in good governance was needed for power groups: the military, the bureaucracy and political parties. Until Indonesian leadership could attain this quality of reform-mindedness, democracy would be out of reach. Student organisations remained important but, where they spurned bribery, tended to volatile initiatives.

At this point of Megawati's rule at the beginning of year 2003, on the intellectual side at least, political analysis and criticism of leadership had arrived at a certain point of awareness but not practical acceptance. Agitation, implying a shortfall in political maturity, still dominated the scene. One outstanding reason for this agitation was corruption. Another was political opportunism. The agitation against Megawati for her raising of fuel and other prices successfully achieved a result for the agitators. First, the government restored the subvention on telephone charges. Shortly after, it stated that it would restore partial subsidies for fuel and electricity. Apparently the very survival of Megawati's government was being threatened by probably the same ad hoc coalition of forces that had brought Gus Dur into power, and which had quietly but willy-nilly worked with the armed forces to bring Gus Dur down. One can suspect what such a coalition could have done, which consisted of: namely, elements of the so-called *poros tengah*, Amien Rais who could have remained influential with the *poros tengah*, Islamic fundamentalist groups, Suharto New Order figures still powerful in the background, and a grouping of top TNI current and retired generals hailing from all the groupings mentioned. Could it be that history was repeating itself?

What was the agenda of this latest cluster? The media referred to it as an ad hoc coalition of forces. What was this coalition's purpose? Answer: To de-stabilise the administration, or at least to weaken it. This cluster or coalition has been referred to as the "presidium" or "national rescue caucus". Thus the attack on the administration was for the purpose of taking over the reins of government. Was de-stabilisation to precede a coup?

Actually the so-called "national rescue caucus" had been formed the previous December by State Minister for National Development Kwik Kian Gie. The purpose was to bring together "good" people in the DPR. But Kwik stopped being active in the body he had himself formed. The caucus was, so to speak, hijacked by remaining members. These were Golkar, PDI-P, Reform faction, PKB and PPP members. Other important personages were also involved, such as Arifin Panigoro, for example. Panigoro's involvement was an indication that there was interest on the part of Suharto forces.

The presidium notion arose separately, and involved personages like Eros Jarut, leader of the Bung Karno nationalist party, supported by student activist Hariman Siregar, and even former General Wiranto as well as other active and retired generals. It was a fairly mixed bag, and not necessarily homogeneous in political outlook, nor mutually friendly. The discussion, to try to depose Megawati through parliament by claiming popular dissatisfaction with her rule, reportedly arose out of a meeting in which various personalities were present.

As Amien Rais was reported to have remarked, the doors and windows to such a parliamentary outcome were closed. Because the play was for high stakes, many participated in the match, probably because they did not want to be left out of the game. Megawati herself joined in by defying those that were looking for a non-constitutional short cut to meet her in the 2004 elections.

The "game" was however one that could have historic consequences. Megawati took seriously enough the briefing she received from her chief of intelligence, Hendropriyono, to haul back from proceeding with the fuel and other price rises, as if twisting away from a cobra strike. The game apparently had its knightly aspects. Megawati celebrated her birthday by urging, before a few hundred of her supporters, that those opposed to her should face her at the polls in 2004. Among the gifts she received was a bouquet of flowers from General Wiranto.

# CHAPTER 23

---

# A REVIEW OF TERRORISM

HOWEVER one reviewed, as a whole, the genesis and activities of the Laskar Jihad, the acquittal of its chief, Jafar Umar Thalib, of inciting violence between Muslims and Christians came as a surprise. It was also regarded as a setback for the government in its attempts to deal with Islamic extremism and communal violence. Interestingly, two Christian separatist leaders were sentenced to three years' imprisonment.

The judge, in Thalib's case, justified Thalib's actions on the grounds of free speech and righteous defence of Indonesia's unity. In Indonesia, it seemed difficult to associate responsibility on the part of leadership with the excesses of the followers. The military found it so in the case of alleged human rights abuses.

Authorities in Maluku had suggested that allies of former president Suharto could be behind the assault on Maluku by the Laskar Jihad, and therefore were its patrons. Jaffar Umar Thalib was believed to have strong links with members of the former *Orde Baru* regime. Its connection with the elite was pointed out as the reason the Laskar Jihad could so easily be transported from Java to Maluku. Its connections with the military were also how the LJ got arms and other war, including transport, equipment so easily, and could operate with such impunity.

The question must have risen in people's minds about how the Thalib verdict might affect the case against Abu Bakar Bashir, then on trial for alleged involvement in the 2000 Christmas Eve bombings. There was some ground to show that Thalib and Bashir represented two unevenly separate lines of radical Islamic persuasion. The Laskar Jihad and the Jemaah Islamiyah (JI) were birds of a feather, but did not necessarily roost in the same nest.

On December 28, 2002, Bali police general I Made Pastika declared that the results of the investigation into the Bali bombing should leave no doubt that the Jemaah Islamiyah was alive and well in Indonesia. Probably intelligence quarters had already known that the JI or its sympathisers had conducted instruction in several locations in Indonesia, for small groups to familiarise themselves with use of weapons and bomb-making. Such rank and file later fought, for example, in Maluku and Poso, where fighting experience provided further in-depth training. Thus Maluku and Poso were important breeding grounds for fighters for the JI.

It was baffling why eminent soldier-politicians like Bambang Yudhoyono could, at one time, publicly state their contrary view, namely that JI did not exist in Indonesia. Yudhoyono later withdrew his statement of disbelief. The leadership of JI was suspected to be in the hands of Abu Bakar Bashir, later detained and then arrested and charged. Bashir had deep knowledge of the JI and how it operated. He most likely had pre-knowledge of bombings, particularly the Christmas Eve 2000 bombings. Bashir was charged with involvement in this particular act of terrorism.

The Christmas Eve bombings illustrated how coordinated the JI were. The network delivered nearly 40 bombs to churches or priests in locations extending from Medan, through Sumatra, Riau, Java and Bali to Lombok. Nearly 20 were killed and 120 injured. Although the technical level did not seem very high, the bombing in Batam was close enough to Singapore to raise some consternation. Riau could be used as a launch pad for a terrorist attack on Singapore. As events evolved, Selamat Kastari the head, or *wakalah*, of the Singapore JI was later arrested in Bintan.

Thus, a spread of terrorist cells existed in Indonesia. Certain elements in the military must have been aware of their regional links. The Jemaah Islamiyah was known to have started as a sting operation devised by General Ali Murtopo to lure Darul Islam followers so that they could be chopped. Murtopo was an intelligence genius, much to whose credit could be attributed efforts to end the "*ganjang* Malaysia" activities of Sukarno's Konfrontasi against Malaysia (*ganjang* meant masticate and spit out).

Murtopo must have achieved partial success. Scores of Darul Islam followers were apprehended, but some following of the movement seemed to have survived, particularly in West Java (Tasik Malaya) and South Sumatra (Lampung). Certainly the Jemaah Islamiyah, or important figures in it, continued to be encouraged associates of a covey of Indonesian military officers. A spread (perhaps rather than network) of Islamic radicals was in position even during Suharto's time. After all, the old despot had been uncomfortable under the scrutiny of the Christian Benny Murdani. He therefore initiated a policy of encouraging the emergence of pro-Islamic highly placed officers in ABRI. One of the characteristics in ABRI/TNI might have been that two principal clusters of such officers might be discerned. One continued to favour the original Murtopo-ordained Jemaah Islamiyah. The other produced the Laskar Jihad.

Under a later-evolved JI command, Laskar Jundullah operated in Poso and Maluku under Agus Dwikarna. Agus was later arrested in the Philippines. Laskar Mujahideen, the armed force of the Ngruki network, totalled about

500 men. Both Laskar Jihad and Laskar Mujahidin had separate links to the army in Maluku from whom they rented guns. But the Laskar Jihad were stronger and later claimed they chased the Mujahideen away. This antagonism explains why the Laskar Jihad were ordered by their bosses to quit their fighting in Maluku and Sulawesi: in order not to be confused with the Al Qaeda-related (by this time) Jemaah Islamiyah.

# CHAPTER 24

---

# VIOLENCE AND CONFUSION: INEVITABLE BACKGROUND TO THE 2004 ELECTIONS?

IT WOULD be bizarre to involve the Indonesian military in the most extreme violence that was typified by the Bali bombing. But agents of the TNI elements were certainly responsible for the unrest in Maluku and Sulawesi. There were suspicions that troubles in Irian Jaya (Papua) and even Aceh could have revealed the hand of TNI agents also. Habibie saw TNI-trained militia running riot in East Timor, as punishment for Timor opting for independence from Indonesia. Gus Dur saw the infiltration of Laskar Jihad forces into Maluku and elsewhere. Even Megawati witnessed the engineering of violence and disorder in Indonesia's periphery. Strategists and tacticians of a kind were at work to demonstrate how much the strong arm of the military's influence in government was needed.

The Bali Bombing made the segment of the military responsible for internecine conflict call off their Muslim jihadist militia. The military did not want their own hounds to be identified with Islamic Jemaah Islamiyah and Al Qaeda terrorists. That was why, in the early confusion after the Bali Bombing, some top figures – even one like Susilo Bambang Yudhoyono – in Indonesia's leadership denied for a brief while that there were terrorists in Indonesia. Such ambivalence continued to prevail, as evidenced in some of the sentencing Indonesian courts were disposed to hand out to terrorist criminals. Then there were prominent government figures (as exemplified by Vice-President Hamzah Haz) who spoke with the same tongue as convicted extremists (like Abu Bakar Bashir) – namely that the US was the real terrorist, principally because it supported Israel.

The indigenous bombers of Indonesia were treated with an uncertain and conflicting orientation. The anti-West, anti-capitalist propaganda statements (in court!) of key Bali suspect Mukhlas show a studied defence based on terrorist teachings. Aspects of this were bound to evoke sympathy for the philosophical stance, even if not for the person. A book sold freely in Jakarta exposed the JI network's organisation and training. It was called "*Gerilya*" and showed the JI set-up and grooming of its fighters to be sophisticated and lethal.

Malaysia was intending to release Mohamad Iqbal Abdul Rahman, a suspected JI leader, for his return to Indonesia. There were no charges yet against Mohamad Iqbal in Indonesia, where he might go free. In regard to Iraq, the popular view prevailed that US action was anti-Arab, and constituted a grab for oil. Hassan Wirajuda, Indonesia's Foreign Minister, criticised the US for its actions in Iraq. He said that military operations created martyrs, and facilitated recruitment campaigns of terrorists. Ali Alatas, former Indonesian foreign minister, called for a better understanding of Islam. It had to be seen, even after Saddam Hussein's dramatic capture, how much such widely held views would be affected.

It was a pity that influential generals in the military entertained suspicions that the West was seeking to weaken the TNI and bring about the downfall of Indonesian society and polity. The multi-dimensional crisis Indonesia was experiencing had triggered a lamentable paradigm change in the political, economic and security situation. It was threatening to push Indonesia 50 years backwards. There was strong implication that all that had been achieved by Suharto would be lost. Indonesians themselves observed that the Suharto regime tolerated corruption, but it was pyramidal. But in the era of *demokrasi* and *reformasi*, corruption permeated the whole society, uncontrollably, affecting all aspects of Indonesian life, because the pyramid had collapsed.

In the dismayed eyes of Indonesia's military leaders, *demokrasi* appeared hollow, as against the euphoric and unfulfilled expectations of the ordinary people. I observed that sort of phenomenon in Moscow, after Gorbachev's downfall. Many Muscovites compared their predicament with how better off they seemed during the Soviet regime. But the Russians recovered. Can the Indonesians do the same?

The heart of the matter, if one wants to consider the military as holding the key to restoring order in Indonesia, is that the military must be induced to reform itself. During Gus Dur's time, a liberal TNI star – Letjen Agus Wirahadikusumah – blazed for a while. But his radical reform programme evoked dismay within the military. Agus WK wanted to run down the territorial system and abolish ABRI's dual function, which allowed the military to spread its tentacles right into the heart of the countryside. He also uncovered a financial scandal in Kostrad, and proposed audits for businesses run by various military units.

Most generals acknowledged that the earthquake in their midst was actually a remarkably intelligent soldier. But he was too far ahead of his time.

A sudden (some say, unauthorised) trip to Washington added to Agus WK's maverick image. Agus WK died suddenly of a mysterious heart attack. Many must have mingled a sigh of relief with their sighs of condolence. But the seed of TNI reform was germinating slowly. The question was how to encourage that growth and assist it. It was not impossible for the TNI to undergo such a paradigm change as would enable it to play the role it has historically figured for itself – that of the nation's saviour.

Against such a background to the final approach of the 2004 elections, a bomb attack took place on September 9 against the Australian Embassy in Jakarta. Nine people were killed and over 180 injured. However, because the deaths and injuries affected mostly Indonesian people, would Megawati's administration be looked on in a poorer light? Would the image in people's minds of Megawati's impotence worsen? As it was she did not do remarkably well against Susilo Bambang Yudhoyono in the first run of the elections.

# Ryamizard Ryacudu

A dominant, expressive figure in this dramatic period of Indonesia's history was army chief General Ryamizard Ryacudu. This unusually named but highly placed military personality is not named here as a potential politician, much less someone for the presidency. But he sees himself as influencing the peaceful outcomes of the election process. This army chief frequently declared that Indonesia had no choice but to remain a unitary state. He stated in a *Time* interview (May 26, 2002) that no region would be allowed to break away. Apparently, in Indonesia's population of 220 million, those provinces even numbering up to a million would have to remain within the unitary framework.

The general also said (*Sinar Harapan,* 22 December 2003) that there was no dichotomy between the civilian and military (segments of Indonesian society). The integration between the two was absolute and unconditional. The spirit of the army was what ensured such essential unity. The separation of the armed forces from the *rakyat* would spell doom for the nation, and must be resisted. Indonesians had also to be aware of the interference in the affairs of the country by foreign forces sowing internal conflict.

In *Inside Indonesia* (April – June 2003) Ed Aspinall reported that after the Bali bombing, Ryamizard Ryacudu gave an order for "the intelligence network to be re-opened". Apparently, he had in mind the retention of the military's territorial structure. Ryacudu was a hardliner, but not such that he was not thinking also of reform for the military.

With regard to the elections, if there were bloody incidents, the TNI would prefer the elections department and police to handle the situation. The army would descend only if the country were threatened with break-up. The military were not thirsty for power, and had no desire to be dragged into peace-keeping during elections, said the general, (who was son-in-law of Try

Sutrisno) giving a warning to political parties to behave.

# New Parties

Among the stars (mostly film) flashing out of the blue, was Siti Hardiyanti Rukmana, Sukarno's daughter known familiarly as Tutut. The announcement (in December 2003) of Tutut as challenger in the 2004 presidential elections evoked a gathering view that she may well be a formidable figure, a promise that turned out to be unfulfilled.

Apparently a new party had been formed, known as the Concern for the Nation Functional Party. It was retired general Raden Hartono, former army chief, who had set up the party. His close official and personal relations with the Suharto family could prompt people to ask what the plan was. Other leading politicians in the race gamely stated that it was up to the people to choose the president they wanted.

But the curiosity surrounding Hartono's party was further stimulated by reports of Megawati's sister, Rachmawati, threatening to enter the presidential race and Sukmawati (the youngest daughter of Sukarno) promising to support her and wanting to down eldest sister Megawati. Rachmawati headed a marhaenist party. Marhaenism was a Sukarnoist concept, which passionately supported the rights of farmers, workers and the poor.

Rachmawati was a frequent and active critic of Megawati's lackadaisical orientation when it was displayed. The two Sukarno daughters' agitation, especially the Marhaenist content of their instigation, could well sour support for Megawati. But who were they for? They wanted the spotlight for themselves, obviously. But observers assessed that Rachmawati's chances were not excessively good. It was interesting to note that Tutut Suharto, when she was social affairs minister in her father's last cabinet, ordered the distribution of coupons for free food among the poor. Was this a display of her Marhaenist orientation? However, appearing as ballast against the pro-Suharto forces, which were beginning to emerge into prominence, there was some excited urging, particularly from Megawati's Indonesian Democratic Struggle Party (PDI-P), that investigations should be resumed into Suharto's wealth.

On on the other hand, there was evidence surfacing that people were getting fed up with corruption, crime and a collapsing infrastructure – congested roads, poor sewerage and environmental conditions, ever deteriorating housing conditions, collapsing law and order situations, rising costs – all threatening growth and development. For the media had actually reported (*The Straits Times* – 3.12.03) that Indonesia's infrastructure, exemplified by piped water, sewerage, electricity, basic housing, was in a critical, parlous condition.

It was like Russia where, during Gorbachev's time of striving after reform, both suffering proletariat and country dwellers hankered after previous communist rule. In Indonesia, the *rakyat* had become amnesiac over the excesses of the Suharto regime, remembering the better basic livelihood they had enjoyed compared with their current continuous suffering. The Marhaen wanted little, and even that little they could not get in the so-called era of *reformasi* and *demokrasi*.

In such a time of uncertainty, there would be at least a few cynical but realistic observers who remembered the way Abdurrahman Wahid had come into the presidency, and also the method of the unseating of Gus Dur to enable Megawati to take over. Shrewd observers would ask what the political game was this time. Would they put their finger on the TNI quotient?

There would be many figures who would represent this quotient, and would include those from the military who were in office as ministers, and would have therefore shed their uniforms. But the most prominent name was that of Wiranto. Could it be that Wiranto was the real focus of the behind-the-scenes conspiring? And could Tutut be one of the more important tokens in reducing Megawati's popular majority. Or would there be someone else coming from really out of the blue like Prabowo Subianto? This could be only if Prabowo had made his peace with Wiranto and the Suharto family.

The Suharto name still had a powerful, reverential hold over the popular imagination. And this was shown by the reportedly larger crowds and greater festive air at the Suharto clan's residence when Aidil Fitri 2003 was celebrated, than at the presidential palace. Whatever may be the condition of rivalry between the two historical "houses" of Sukarno and Suharto, there seemed greater cohesion in the Suharto family than in the inheritors of the Sukarno name. But this was in the background.

The real challenge to Megawati would still come from a military figure. This writer was still plonking for Wiranto. He had come to Singapore on a publicity programme, and had autographed two of his publications for me. His was a powerful persuasive stance. Later when he won the Golkar nomination, even against Golkar's chief Akbar Tandjung, his chances appeared even brighter.

I was persuaded to feel supportive towards Wiranto. I was reacting against a strong inclination of certain supporters of Megawati to summon past statistics, showing Megawati's previous electoral strength, as a foretaste of Megawati's winning chances in the 2004 presidential elections. I totally disagreed with such a hidebound and unimaginative prediction. It displayed an unpreparedness for a paradigm change. But I too was wrong about Wiranto.

# CHAPTER 25

# SUSILO BAMBANG YUDHOYONO

BEHIND the aspirations of Megawati Sukarnoputri and General Wiranto, and the ambitions and would-be role-playing of new upstart parties, one name was being mentioned as someone to note. But not only as someone to note, but as a very likely successful candidate for the presidency. This someone, who was gradually but soon confidently described as the front-runner, was Susilo Bambang Yudhoyono, popularly referred to as SBY.

Precisely when Wiranto won the Golkar nomination, Jusuf Kalla, wealthy businessman from Sulawesi, dropped out of Golkar. He teamed up with SBY, as SBY's V-P nominee. Public opinion polls persistently proclaimed Bambang as the front-runner. There was gathering conviction after the first election run-off that Bambang would be the main challenger and probable victor in the second and final trial.

The early modest projection of Susilo Bambang Yudhoyono's political image was deceptive. Despite SBY's win in the first round of the presidential elections, on July 5, with one-third of the total votes going to him, while Megawati scored about one-fourth, Bambang acted as if his final victory against incumbent Megawati was yet to be certain. Who would immediately decide on his odds, coming as he did from a small minority party? But the quiet self-confidence of the man was amazing.

The surprisingly versatile Bambang was not averse to using the same pop music approach as Wiranto. In fact the latter even admitted that Bambang was better than Wiranto himself in the early hustings. But in a quotable quote, Bambang was credited with saying that socialisation of the archipelago required a good singer, not only a good song. The reality remained that Bambang's personal popularity ouweighed his rivals' organisational superiority.

Bambang's was a simple matter-of-fact approach. How was he so quietly self-assured in anticipating who would win over the voters? One clue was to study how he set out his ideas, shortly after Gus Dur had made Bambang a coordinating minister. Singapore bureau chief for Business Week, Michael Shari, asked the questions (*BusinessWeek Online,* 11 September 2000), and Bambang gave thoughtful, straightforward, but illuminating answers.

SBY's image can perhaps be better discerned when compared with that of Wiranto. General Wiranto had aroused persistent antagonism in East Timor, as one who, at least, did nothing to stop the depredations of the Indonesian armed forces, and their militia, after the little island had opted for independence from Indonesia. Internationally, too, Wiranto as president would be an embarrassment that was difficult to overcome.

SBY's was an image of thoughtful integrity, of one who refused to go along with a suggestion by Gus Dur, that he should declare a state of emergency, in order to save the situation for the half blind president. Gus Dur had chalked up a trail of inconsistencies and authoritarian decisions. Bambang, who had stayed by Gus Dur's side as long as he could, lost his job as security minister. He also lost his job when he quarrelled with President Megawati, towards the end of her regime.

At the same time, his were strategic actions, bolstered by fallback positions readily available because of his known ability. Sacked by Gus Dur, SBY was quickly accepted by Megawati's camp; and quarrelling with Megawati, SBY steadied himself to take part in the presidential elections. What was clear was that SBY was not ready to sacrifice his honest conclusions for the sake of ambition and position.

How to explain Susilo Bambang Yudhoyono's lead in the polls, and his emergence as president-elect? SBY did not have a big party machine, totally unlike the PDI-P-Golkar coalition that was supposed to act together in support of Megawati. This could be the paradigm shift in the Indonesian elections, and indeed in the total Indonesian outlook. Possibly such a shift was assisted by the in-fighting that was reported to be going on *within* each of the the two parties as well as *between* them.

When the time came Bambang, echoing what he had told Michael Shari, reiterated his careful promise of determined rule and clean government. Bambang showed himself to be ever cautious. He needed to mull over matters, before reaching a conclusion. He said at first there were no terrorists in Indonesia. But he swiftly corrected himself after Bali.

Bambang's popularity seemed to burgeon after he left Megawati in March 2004. He became the Democratic Party's presidential candidate. He swiftly chose Jusuf Kalla as his running mate. This clever choice was a quick decision, which showed Bambang could think on his feet when necessary. But it could also reflect astute Javanese pre-planning.

As a Javanese, SBY needed a figure to balance against the image of Javanese colonialism which SBY by himself might present. Sukarno himself had chosen Mohammed Hatta. Indeed Megawati chose Hamzah Haz. But, over and above the fact that Jusuf Kalla was from Sulawesi, he was also one of the wealthiest men in Indonesia. He did not need to look around for stray pickings.

However, one important factor in voter preference for SBY was that, while voters followed party lines in the legislative elections, they apparently did not do so in the first run-off to the presidential elections. Instead it *seemed* to be according to voters' perception of candidates' abilities. They certainly ignored the clamour of party urgings. Apparently an effective majority had faith that Susilo Bambang Yudhoyono could solve the country's manifold problems

In his choice of Jusuf Kalla, Bambang thought of the Muslim constituency, although he had to balance this against Christian votes in East Indonesia. Was the backing given to Bambang by Yusril Ihza Mahendra and his Crescent Star Party, and others, a sign that the *poros tengah*, which had so powerfully put Gus Dur in *his* election to the presidency, was also favouring SBY?

In the midst of the euphoria (on the expected winning side, at least), pessimistic warning voices seem to have faded into the background. One such voice could point that a bit of democracy and still a lot of backwardness formed a gloomy backdrop to the presidential elections. *REPUBLIKAonline* (Tuesday, 13 July 2004) published the urgings of university professor Syahruddin who appealed to the people not to place too much hope on a new president. The people should stand on their own resources. Syahruddin implied that it was too much to expect that a new government would be able, without difficulty, to overcome the economic crisis, which had been riddling society for years, and provide enjoyment of an atmosphere of peace and prosperity – just like that.

Still, certain parties were not above making all sorts of promises. Megawati's people were talking as if she seemed certain to win the elections. They promised that, if the Mega-Hasyim team won, Mega would form a cabinet, which was clean, effective and oriented towards the *rakyat*. Mega would not choose any minister or assistant who would be irresponsible, and who would leave his unfinished job halfway. This last bit could have been a dig at Susilo Bambang Yudhoyono. She also assured the public that she would not display any leanings towards the military. She guaranteed press freedom and democracy. Such were brave words, but they were too late.

Megawati self-consciously referred to a "rainbow" cabinet, which was how her cabinet had been hopefully described. Since the constitution would not allow her another shot at the presidency, she could not entertain herself with thoughts of the 2009 elections. So the interests of the *rakyat* would shine through a regime, which could not sport such an agenda. Such thoughts were reported in the *Harian Berita Sore* (13.7.04).

Bambang merely promised that he would refuse to enter into a bargain, *dagang sapi* (in other words, cattle trading) with other parties over cabinet places. He would wait until after the elections to seek cooperation with Parliament or the administration. Bambang showed a cool efficiency when he served both Gus Dur and Megawati. His few foes tried to show him in poor light when he left both Gus Dur and Megawati.

But he had played a dominant role in Gus Dur's regime. After quickly recovering from the shock of the Bali bombing, Bambang played a leading role in action against terrorists, acknowledged both at home – where the Mega government appeared inactive – but more particularly also in the international scene. One can only wonder at the reason for Bambang's quarrel with Megawati and her husband resulting in his resignation in March 2004. Immediately after this, SBY declared his ambitions for the Indonesian presidency.

Bambang's most important task, after assuming the presidency, would be to confidently set right Indonesia's economic stance. He can expect good-neighbourly help from Singapore. When times and things were previously not so good, Singapore investments in Indonesia were yet significant. The Singapore newspaper *Today* (4.10.04) pointed to SingTel acquiring stakes in Indonesia's largest cellular phone company Telcomsel. Temasek Holdings bought stakes in two Indonesian banks.

Still, Yudhoyono has tough foes. Megawati, up to the moment of her review at a ceremony to mark Armed Forces Day, seemed not ready to acknowledge her opponent's electoral victory. *The Straits Times* (6.10.04) quoted Indonesian legislator Fuad Amris remarking that the Javanese mindset made it difficult for Megawati to accept the reality of being defeated by her (one-time) subordinate. What price "democracy"? Actually the forces that could be arrayed against SBY could be a formidable alliance between Megawati and Akbar Tandjung. But word has it that these are in disorder.

# CHAPTER 26

# ANOTHER LOOK AT BAMBANG'S VICTORY

ONE could still persist in asking how was it that, despite such an apparently formidable duo against him, former general Yudhoyono found such a supportive ground. Could it be his reputation as an efficient, straight-foward administrator, and a no-nonsense one at that, during both Gus Dur's and Megawati's time? Does the *rakyat* remain so mindful over a period of time? Could his clean and honest image have just continually dazzled the masses? Or have SBY's guardian angels been holding a continual watch over how voters (finally, two-third of the total number) would show their pleasure and support?

Who were these agents of popular endorsement? After racking one's logical mind, one possible answer emerges. True, much has been made of the military's total retreat from representation in parliament. Yet, with its very last breath, parliament reportedly passed a law assuring the TNI of its continued powerful presence in the *masyarakat*, in the larger society. The pervasive influence of ABRI when it followed the principle of *masok desa* (entering the villages) may not have been exactly the same in 2004 as before in Suharto's *Orde Baru*, but a watered down and reformed, but nevertheless deft version seems to have remained in place for the TNI.

*The Jakarta Post.com* (8.10.04), although expressing its reservations, reported that the regional military offices would be revamped to empower the defence forces and to avoid the abuses committed by the military in the past. A measured form of the territorial command was now in place. The new bill did not demand the dissolution of the territorial command.

While there did not seem to be a genuine paradigm change, the new law called for the huge military participation in business to be rendered progressively more transparent. So the reform suggested intemperately by the late Agus Wirahadikusuma could be more gradually introduced. There were others too like Agus Widjoyo and Ryacudu Ryamizard who, while holding out for TNI's influence, were supporters of reform. Actually, the move towards the re-assertion of military influence started in Gus Dur's time, in reaction to the hopeful leader's attempts to whittle down military influence. Such a movement seemed to have been carried forward (perhaps subtly) during Megawati's regime, seeing her hesitant, indecisive style of rule. Now this evolution seems to have come to the fore.

Now, what has all this got to do with SBY? Certainly, SBY needed an organisation that could face the challenge of the united forces of PDI-P and Golkar, of Megawati and Akbar Tandjung. This organisation could only be the continued presence of the TNI territorial command. Indeed the military had become so quietly influential that it could persuade Megawati and Akbar Tandjung to stand by while the new law extending TNI's influence over the *masyarakat* was being enacted.

Or was the last sentence the whole story? One odd action Megawati Sukarnoputri took was to accept the sudden resignation of Endriartono Sutarto, and immediately appoint Ryamizard Ryacudu as temporary chief of TNI. Besides this *ad interim* position, Ryacudu continued as army chief, and also took over the command of Kostrad, on retirement of the former Strategic Services Command chief Waluyo. Megawati had also promoted, on her own steam, Hendropriyono (head of intelligence) and Hari Sabarno (Coordinating Minister for Political and Security Affairs) to full generals. Were these the final acts of presidential assertion or preemption or both?

Contradictory media reports were not clear whether the Indonesian parliament would or would not ratify the retiring president's decisions. It looks as if observers have to go one full circle to words uttered by Wiranto in his pre-election manifesto "Unite and advance Indonesia". In it he says that the reform process had been conducted in a make-do manner. Weak legal practice had led the nation to a very dangerous condition, namely disharmony and disorientation.

The attempts at reform, for the past five years had not resulted in significant change. Democratization had only been marked by the opening up of political corridors. Issues of concern included (a) lack of legal supremacy, (b) rampant corruption, (c) increased threats to national security, including increased acts of terrorism, (d) national instability, such as degradation of people's welfare.

Such were the problems confronting Yudhoyono, even if enunciated by a rival whom he had beaten. And then there was what commentators had labelled a "hidden agenda" in Megawati's final demarche. Would SBY have responded: "So what is new?" about Mega's attempted preemption?

What did indeed make the news was the fact that Megawati Sukarnoputri would not, and indeed did not, attend the swearing-in ceremony of Dr Yudhoyono, the newly-elected president of Indonesia. Megawati's tantrums were novel and threatening. Perhaps she had all the time thought that she possessed the *wahyu*, the force of mystic power to rule. To be present thus at the accession of her erstwhile subordinate would be like surrendering her *wahyu*.

When Mega's husband Taufik Kiemas – who did attend the ceremony – was queried by the media, he laughed off the questions by saying that he did not want to talk. Reporting the views of an Islamic scholar, *Berita.sore* (20.10.04) said that the former president's act detracted from the quality of eastern culture. But this was from the point of formal good manners, not of mysticism.

Still, at the end of six years of living dangerously, Indonesia found itself headed by its "first professionally qualified president", according to a report by the *International Herald Tribune* on October 21, 2004. The president himself has tried to shape a cabinet of as professionally qualified people as possible. He has called it the United Indonesia cabinet. Megawati called hers a *gotong royong* cabinet. Gus Dur called his a rainbow cabinet.

Dr Yudhoyono has apparently not been able to resist giving a descriptive name to his cabinet, like his two predecessors. But the latter did not last to fulfil the terminology used. Hopefully the new president's will. He has been compelled to make last-minute changes in the naming of one or two of his ministers. One outstanding example is that Yusuf Anwar was designated Finance Minister instead of the initially chosen Sri Mulyani Indrawati. She has been appointed Chairperson of the National Development Planning Agency (*Bappenas*). Her association with the International Monetary Fund apparently disqualified her from the finance portfolio in the eyes of important political figures who numbered among those who were opposed to Indonesia being involved with the IMF. But *Bappenas* should be challenging enough for her skills and international associations.

In terms of the essential portfolios, the United Cabinet looked promising. Others expressed Indonesia's diversity of political and regional interests. One perhaps should not cavil at this, although an expected chorus had done exactly this. Yudhoyono betrayed the soldier in him when he commanded his ministers to stand at ease before he made his speech at the ceremony inducting them to office. Thus one may say jokingly that, in this way, the military was also represented in the Cabinet.

Perhaps he unconsciously recalled that the military represented a powerful constituency. They had played an important role during the six post-Suharto years, which we have described as a period of Indonesia "living dangerously" throughout. The advance or retreat of the military in various phases could be noted in the following key events:

- the deposition of Habibie;
- the support for Megawati to stand for the Vice-President's post;
- the determined opposition to Gus Dur's appointment of unpopular general Agus WK to high military office;
- the stolid refusal to declare a state of emergency as Gus Dur wanted,

leading to his fall; and
- the indifference towards Megawati in the end.

The Islamic constituency was also important during the six years. It was the *poros tengah* that brought Gus Dur to power. It was Gus Dur in disfavour with even his own Muslim constituents that caused him to fall to Megawati's parliamentary action. Muslim radical groups increased their activity during Megawati's regime. Yet it was interesting to note that Laskar Jihad and Front Pembela Islam immediately folded up, when military puppet masters, at the time of the Bali bombing, wanted them to do so.

From the viewpoint of Islamic forces, Megawati's weakness of rule stemmed from political hesitancy, which they attributed to her being a woman. Other analysts noted that she was head of a secularist party at a time when there was a proliferation of Islamic parties. It did not help either that her Vice-President, Hamzah Haz, frequently undermined her authority by cosying up to Islamic radicals.

The amazing thing is, that with all the forces of massive party organisations arraigned against him, Susilo Bambang Yudhoyono won. One, perhaps partial, explanation has to be SBY's Javanese-ness. A well-known Javanese saying explains an important aspect of SBY's personality. It is *rawe-rawe rantas malang-malang putung*. The dictionary (Echols and Shadily) renders this as "strive onward, no matter what". I myself have interpreted it as having a stability of mind that overcomes hindrance.

One can match other Javanese maxims with other SBY qualities. Perhaps the more significant one is *nglurug tanpa bala* – to fight without troops. His were ordinary people, spread all over the country. Their *rasa* (profound feelings) had been invoked in *rakyat* gazing, with resentment and anger focused on rampant corruption, job losses, rising cost of living, degradation of living standards, and alarming signs of economic collapse. Such *rasa* found harmony in Susilo Bambang Yudhoyono's *santosa* – his sense of recollection and self-control. Galvanising the *rakyat* is one thing. But how did SBY organising their energy (or synergy) towards his electoral victory? That is a mystery that will be unravelled in time.

*Menang tanpa ngasorake* demonstrates SBY's gentlemanliness, his *alus*-ness, his generosity towards Megawati, his erstwhile electoral foe, for the phrase means "winning without humiliating". Finally, we cannot close this cultural aspect, without quoting *jer basuki mawa beya*, which roughly means: "If one wants to succeed, he has to pay." Thus the efforts of those factions which supported President Susilo Bambang Yudhoyono need to be recognised.

## THE END

# POSTSCRIPT

In the early hours of December 26, 2004, a massive earthquake (measuring 9 on the Richter scale) rocked North Sumatra. Within half an hour, huge tsunamis of between 10 to 20 metres hit the region's coastal areas, decimating entire villages and laying waste to the Acehnese capital, Banda Aceh. The monster waves – moving at the speed of a jetliner – also devastated parts of Sri Lanka and Thailand, affected Penang and Langkawi in Malaysia, the Indian Ocean island groups like the Maldives, Seychelles and the Nicobar islands, and coastal areas of Africa like Somalia.

The death toll climbed by the hour as the world watched in horror. At the time of writing, it was estimated that more than 160,000 people lost their lives. Sumatra was the most severely hit, with the official death toll at 110,000 and rising. Help to disaster-ridden Aceh was quickly organised, and put in place with blessed speed.

This disaster is a challenge to the new Indonesian leadership returned by the 2004 elections. President Susilo Bambang Yudhoyono is no doubt facing one of the hardest moments in his political career, even as aid pours in from all parts of the globe.

Just as northern Sumatra may well be seen as a *tabula rasa* on which reconstruction work has to be started almost from scratch, there may also be an element of fresh opportunity in the Indonesian polity itself, and in its relations with other countries, to be taken advantage of. Throngs and clusters of those of negative political leanings and the source of division in the country have a chance of looking away from their own pre-occupations, and upon the tremendous havoc nature has inflicted on their brothers in Indonesia. This natural calamity way well be the challenge of a lifetime for all who love the country of their birth.

## Historic crises in Indonesia's past

Indonesia has had its share of troubles. The major ones are listed here:
- **1883**: Krakatoa, a volcanic island, erupts. The explosion is heard as far away as Australia, thousands of miles away, and its effects are felt throughout the whole world. The particles the volcano throws up surrounds the earth

with darkness. It takes two years for the atmosphere to settle down. The explosion causes tsunami of almost 40 meters high to repeatedly strike the shores of both Java and Sumatra, as well as several other parts of the world. The colossal waves carry rocks, ships and houses deep inland. It is estimated that 36,000 people were killed, a very large figure for a time of smaller populations and lower distributions.

• **1963:** Gunung Agung, the highest mountain in Bali, exploded in 1963. The disaster was one of the world's largest in the 20th century, killed many and destroyed vast tracts of cultivated land. The eruption took between 1,100 and 2,000 lives, although this figure could be an underestimate, but miraculously spared the sacred temple at Besakih.

• **1965:** One of Indonesia's most horrific human disasters could well be the *Gestapu* massacre of September 30. Even today, it is not clearly known who the prime movers of that event were. Certainly, several generals were brutally assassinated. This was followed by a frenzied, country-wide pogrom against those considered communist perpetrators or pro-communist supporters. Hundreds of thousands were killed, and rivers ran red with blood. The full extent of the damage in lives cannot be clearly calculated. But the country eventually recovered.